FINDING FREEDOM

ULF EKMAN

Word of Life Publications

Ulf Ekman Ministries Ltd.
PO Box 2324 Mansfield
QLD 4122 AUSTRALIA

FINANCIAL FREEDOM
First published in English, 1989
Second edition, 1993

ISBN 91 7866 139 0
ISBN 1 884017 05 3 USA

Original Swedish edition, copyright © 1989
Ulf Ekman. All rights reserved

English translation, copyright © 1989 Ulf Ekman

Printed in Finland for Word of Life Publications
by TryckPartner AB

Word of Life Publications
Box 17, S-751 03 Uppsala, Sweden
Box 46108, Minneapolis, MN 55446, USA
Box 641, Marine Parade, Singapore 9144

Acknowledgements
Unless otherwise indicated, Scripture quotations are from
the *New King James Version* of the Bible, copyright ©
1979, 1980, 1982 by Thomas Nelson Publishers, Inc.
Used by permission

Scripture quotations noted NIV are from the *Holy Bible,
New International Version,* copyright © 1973, 1978, 1984
International Bible Society. Used by permission of
Zondervan Bible Publishers

Scripture quotations noted AMP are taken from *The
Amplified Bible,* copyright © 1954, 1958 The Lockman
Foundation

Scripture quotations noted KJV are taken from the *King
James Version* of the Bible

Contents

Introduction

The truth about financial prosperity is an important revelation from the Word of God. For years, it has been concealed because of human thinking and religious traditions. This wrong thinking, which is not based on God's Word, has caused many Christians to miss the plan of God in their finances. They have thought that God was not interested in that part of their lives or that He wanted them to be poor and in need.

The truth is that God is concerned about every area of human life. He has made total provision for those who have given their lives to Christ, by believing in Him and desiring to follow Him. There is no area of our lives that has remained untouched by the death of Jesus at Calvary. Through His death, abundant life and blessing have been made available to us. The goodness of God covers every aspect of human existence and His blessings touch every area, for those who are partakers of His covenant.

It is interesting that as soon as a hidden Biblical truth is brought into the light, a dispute arises. Often those whom the Lord has first instructed regarding the truth, undergo tremendous attack, and there is often a long struggle before the truth eventually becomes established. Once established, however, the entire Body of Christ is able to enjoy it. It has always been this way.

The enemy resists the truth about financial prosperity, intensely. His goal is to bind up the army of God in these last days so that it lacks ammunition, weapons, food and the provisions it needs to accomplish what it is called to do. If Satan succeeds, he has won the war.

It was challenging, to say the least, when the Lord began to raise up teachers to present God's view of money and to allow the anointing on the message of financial prosperity to flow.

We must realize that one of Satan's forces in this world is money; the fear of not having enough money and the greed for more of it. Wherever you go you will find people dictated to and ruled by money. The only exceptions are those who are ruled by the Spirit of God. There are also many people who though not directly ruled by money itself, are ruled by what it can buy.

As believers, we are beginning to learn that God is to have control over our money. Our God is the One who says, *The silver is mine and the gold is mine* (Hag 2:8). This is something that annoys the devil. He realizes that if he loses his control of money, he will lose his control of people.

We must destroy the fear of money. There is nothing inherently wrong with it. There is, however, something wrong with those who are greedy and driven by it. Money itself is not the root of all evil; the *love* of money is a root of all evil (see 1 Tim 6:10).

Unfortunately though, the Body of Christ has thrown "the baby out with the bath water." We are virtually afraid of speaking about money. Why? Because we are fearful that others will think we are overly interested in it. Therefore, we have almost renounced money altogether.

As a result, we have not had the necessary funds to do what we are called to do. This is just what the devil wants. He may be able to trap a few

Christians with greed, but he is more eager to make them afraid of having anything to do with money, even to the point that just talking about it, makes them feel guilty.

It is vital that you recognize the traditions of men concerning this issue. You need to see how these traditions have infiltrated and robbed the Church of God, keeping God's children in financial bondage. Thus, we become easy prey for the enemy in these last days.

Financial prosperity is certainly not a get-rich-quick scheme; however, it does seek to challenge incorrect beliefs concerning money. This teaching about money should be seen in light of the fact that we are living in the last days and in a time when God is restoring and equipping His army. Victory in this area will make it possible for us to spread the Gospel around the world.

Money is a sensitive subject. For many, it is an open wound they dare not touch, think about or speak about. It is vital, however, that we do just this and expose wrong religious thinking. Then we will see people set free. You have not been called to live in financial bondage. You have been redeemed from the curse of the law, a curse which also included poverty (see Gal 3:13; Deut 28).

Poverty consciousness has become such a normal part of people's thinking that it is necessary to renew our minds with the Word of God in this area. It may sometimes take years before this wrong poverty thinking is purged from our minds. However, the Lord wants people to be free to enjoy His blessings in this area.

Sometimes people say, "You have to be balanced." What do they mean by this? It is obvious that we should be balanced, but the only true balance is found in the Word of God. A "balance" of 50% faith and 50% unbelief is not balance at all. This is imbalance. When we are in a state of true balance, the world will regard us as completely unbalanced. Still, many Christians try to appear balanced in the world's eyes in order to gain its acceptance.

If we strive to maintain God's balance, the world will be attracted to us as they see what our God has done for us. This is why it is so important that we do not flirt with the world or compromise with old religious thinking and traditions. We must put things in order so that we can more easily lead the world into the Kingdom of God.

Receive the message of financial prosperity. It does not center on you, instead, it is about being a channel for God's blessings to others.

PART I

FINANCIAL PROSPERITY IN THE OLD TESTAMENT

1

God's Character—Riches and Abundance

And my God shall supply all your need according to his riches in glory by Christ Jesus (Phil 4:19).

Financial prosperity is not just another subject—it is an integral part of the character of God. His character determines the quality of spiritual life you and I enjoy. Therefore, the more you know God, the fewer problems you will have with areas like healing, the authority of the believer, demons, speaking with other tongues, and so on. These will all fall into their rightful place when you see who God actually is. Therefore, we must always return to the foundation—God's character.

The Bible speaks clearly about the nature of our God. Paul shows us something about God's character in his letter to the Philippians. He thanks the believers in Philippi for blessing him with their money and other gifts. He tells them that because they have given to him, God will also meet their needs. "My God is rich," he says. "My God will meet every one of your needs."

Notice that the scripture does not say that God will give you just enough to break even. It does not even say that He carefully evaluates and measures out according to your needs. It says that He sees your needs, and meets them according to His riches—not just according to the amount of your need.

God does not measure His giving as we do. Ephesians 3:20 says He gives *exceedingly abundantly above all that we ask or think.* He gives much more than you think He should give. He gives according to His riches because He is a rich God. He gives in full measure, just as it says in Luke 6:38: *Give, and it will be given to you: good measure, pressed down, shaken together, and running over will be put into your bosom.*

To give in good measure means to give abundantly. It means using a larger measure than is really necessary—the largest measure one has. "Pressed down" means packing the measure as full as possible, then shaking it together to add a little more. Finally, when the measure is completely full, even more is added until it ends up running over.

Give and it will be given to you: good measure, pressed down, shaken together, and running over!

And my God shall supply all your need according to his riches in glory by Christ Jesus (Phil 4:19).

God enjoys giving. Just as you enjoy giving gifts to others, He enjoys giving to you. God is a cheerful giver.

Many people believe that they have to nag and beg God to give them something, until He finally says, "OK, here, take this and be quiet" just to get rid of them. Some even make the mistake of raising their children in this way.

However, God is not like that. He is eager to give things to you and He does it cheerfully. He loves to give, both because He is rich and because, according to John 3:16, He is a giver by nature.

For God so loved the world, the Bible tells us, *that He gave His only begotten Son....* This verse is important in showing us the character of God. You need to see His character with regard to giving so that you will no longer have a bad conscience in this area.

God is a Giver

God has two primary characteristics in the area of giving: first, He is a rich God and second, He is a glad and cheerful giver. God loves to give. He gave the best and most precious thing He had to give, and He was deeply involved in His giving. We know that Jesus said, *The thief does not come except to steal, and to kill, and to destroy. I have come that they may have life, and that they may have it more abundantly* (John 10:10). We see from this scripture that God is involved in giving and the devil is involved in stealing.

There is a religious way of thinking which says that God does not give everything He has, because we are unable to manage it properly. Instead, we are told, He saves His blessings until we are old or until we get to heaven. This is wrong.

If I am unable to manage finances, it may be because not everything in my life is pleasing to God. If this is so, God wants to help me put my life in order so that I can use His blessings correctly. But He is not withholding them because He is afraid I cannot handle them.

The Bible reveals to us that God is wealthy; there are streets of gold and gates made of pearls in heaven. There is no deficiency there because God is in heaven, and heaven is a perfect and complete reflection of His character. You can read a description of heaven in the Book of Revelation. There is gold and crystal, and diamonds and pearls without end.

If being rich is a sin, then God is the greatest of all sinners. This is the logical conclusion of such absurd thinking! God is rich. He lives in abundance in every area. His life is an abundant one and it is this life He has given us through His Son, Jesus Christ.

Get Used to the Word of God

There are people who are afraid to use the word "money," and others who feel the same about the word "rich." However, the word "rich" is often used in the Bible. Often, though not always, it is used to refer directly to money. You should get used to using the Word of God without being ashamed. You need to be balanced and to avoid either extreme, but you should not be ashamed of the scriptures.

You need to be able to use words found in the Bible without feeling embarrassed. You will gain nothing by diluting God's Word, so don't waste your time trying to please those who will end up not believing what you say anyway. Say what God says, no more and no less. It is the truth that sets people free.

God revealed Himself to Abraham in Genesis 17:1 by saying, *I am Almighty God; walk before me and be blameless. And I will make My covenant between Me and you, and will multiply you exceedingly.*

The word translated "Almighty" in this verse is the Hebrew word *El Shaddai*. This word may give us the impression that God is great, almighty and far away. Words can give us both right and wrong associations. The words "El Shaddai," however, not only mean almighty and great, they also mean "the God of abundance."

Abundance is the state of having more than enough. When you are in abundance you have enough left over to give to others. God is almighty and omnipotent and has more than enough for all of us.

"El Shaddai" actually means "the many breasted One." Strange though it may sound, this is its literal meaning. God gives life in the same way that a mother's breast gives life and nourishment to a newly born child. The word, therefore, has this combined meaning, that God gives more than enough. He *is* more than enough. He is the God who gives life and abundance. This is our God.

God Has Made a Covenant with You

God made a covenant with Abraham. In so doing, He placed at Abraham's disposal all that He had and was able to do. Through Christ Jesus, you too have become a part of this covenant. When you are in need, as you often are, you know that He is greater than your needs and that He has bound Himself to meet every one of them.

God is bound by His Word. Some people say, "But you cannot force God to do something." Yes, you can. This may sound extreme, but it is exactly what God has said. This is the nature of a covenant; but it must not be confused with a carnal and demanding attitude.

Let's look at Mark 11:24: *Whatever things you ask when you pray, believe that you receive them, and you will have them.* The word "ask" here is *aiteo*, which means "demand" in the original text. It is a very strong word and therefore it is interesting to note that Jesus used it.

To "demand," as the Bible uses the word, is different from jumping up and down and shouting out demands. It is boldly knowing what God has said and that He has made a covenant with us in which He has placed everything at our disposal. God has taken the initiative, not us. He has committed Himself through the covenant and has put all that He has at our disposal. How can we know what this actually means? By understanding who He is—the God of abundance.

God could choose to keep His abundance for Himself. After all, He is God and can do whatever He wishes. If He wanted, He could say to us, "You're not getting anything. You should be grateful that I even let you into my Kingdom." Indeed we should be happy that we have been accepted in the Kingdom of God.

The prodigal son (see Luke 15) realized that his father's servants were better off than he was. So he said, "I am not worthy to be called your son. I'll do anything as long as you let me come home again." We too should rejoice that we can do the same; we can come to our Father's house and know that we will be accepted.

Think about this—what if God had said, "I am not helping you with a thing. I'm not healing a single sickness. You'll just have to stumble your way through life." Would we still shout hallelujah? I would, because I am not saved in order to get earthly blessings; I'm saved in order to escape from hell and to spend eternity in heaven.

However, this is not the nature of our God and it is wrong of us to suggest that He is like this. We should do nothing but gratefully receive what He has already promised. Through His covenant with us, the Almighty God has placed His abundance at our disposal. This is the meaning of a covenant.

But before this covenant blessing can become a manifested reality in your life, you must put yourself at God's disposal. Until you have done this the covenant will not work for you. Just as God has put everything at our disposal, we must put everything at His.

One day God may tell you, "I need your arms, or I need your tongue, or I need your eyes, your legs, your life, your money or your family. I have a need, and I want to make a covenant with you. Whenever I am in need of something on earth, I want you to put yourself at my disposal. When I need your hands, I want you to give them to me. When I need your mouth, I want you to give it to me. I want you to give me your time when I need it." We must accept this as our part of the covenant.

This is what it means to have Jesus as Lord. It is walking in forgiveness for our sins and in the righteousness of God, which has been provided for us in Christ Jesus. It is realizing that all God owns has been made available to us, and that you can take advantage of His abundance when in need of it. However, it also means that when God needs your hands to heal, you must be willing to lay them on the sick for Him.

God Keeps His Promises

God is more than willing to meet your every need through the covenant He has made with you. The truth is, He is actually obligated to meet your needs.

He has obligated Himself with His covenant. He could just as well have said that He would not give us anything and in that case He would have no obligations. But because He has said the opposite, He has bound Himself to His promises.

When the theological seas run high in a discussion of this sort, I always like to quote what Luther said, "Fill God's ears with His own promise and force Him to do what He has promised." You can remind God of what He has said, because He is a covenant-keeping God, and He wants to do what He has promised. He is the God of abundance who abundantly gives us all that we need.

> Blessed be the God and Father of our Lord Jesus Christ, who has blessed us with every spiritual blessing in the heavenly places in Christ (Eph 1:3).

God has truly blessed us. Some say that this applies only to "spiritual" and not material blessings, but this is only because they have not understood the true meaning of the word "spiritual." The long-term influence of Greek philosophy has twisted their understanding of the scriptures. We see in the Old Testament that whatever comes from God is considered spiritual. The Bible never puts the spiritual in opposition to the material. **Anything that comes from God, who is a spirit, is to be considered spiritual.**

Unfortunately, Greek philosophy crept into the Church in the form of Gnosticism, which differentiates between the inner, spiritual life and the outward, material one. The outward life was said to be evil and, in order for one to be truly spiritual, it had to be denounced. Cloisters and monasteries arose in which people flagellated themselves and took oaths of poverty in an attempt to win God's acceptance. But it was a doctrine of works.

The Body of Christ is still suffering the after effects of this kind of thinking today. This is how the poverty mentality entered the Church. But God does not separate the spiritual from the material. He created the whole man and consequently He always blesses the whole man.

The Lord—My Provider

Genesis 22 describes how Abraham did not withhold his only son, Isaac, but was willing to offer him to God. On the way up the mountain in the land of Moriah, Isaac asked Abraham where the offering was. Abraham replied by saying, *God will provide for himself the lamb for a burnt offering* (v. 8). Then in verse 14 we read that Abraham named the place "The Lord Will Provide."

The Hebrew word translated in English as "the Lord will provide" is *Jehovah Jireh*. In English we use the verb "provide," although a more accurate translation would be "the Lord is the provider." This is a proper name in Hebrew, the Lord my Provider, and is one of the seven covenant names in the Old Testament which reveal the character of God.

It is interesting to notice that the name of God that follows "El Shaddai," the God of Abundance, is "Jehovah Jireh," the Lord my Provider. In other words, this is the second name God uses to reveal Himself.

Look what happened when the children of Israel were about to leave Egypt. The first thing God did as He led them out, was to make sure they took the gold and silver belonging to the Egyptians. He provided for them. This is one of the first and most important revelations of God's character. While leaving Egypt He also said, *I am the Lord who heals you* (Ex 15:26).

Here we can see provision and healing as the primary revelations of the true nature of God. The devil, probably more than anything else, has tried desperately to hide these aspects of God's character from the Body of Christ. The fact is, though, that the Lord is our provider. He is the God of abundance. God is a rich God and He is a cheerful giver.

These truths are revealed to us through God's names. Because His name is the God who Heals, He does heal, cure and restore. Because His name is the Lord your Provider, He does provide for you, in accordance with His abundance and glorious riches in Christ Jesus. This is the eternal and unchanging nature of God.

Get to Know God!

It is important that you receive a revelation of the character of God from His Word. Through understanding God's character and covenant, you will begin to understand how He thinks. And this understanding is important.

There may be situations in your everyday life when you need to know the will of God, but are unable to find a scripture that applies to your specific situation. However, if you know God's Word and are acquainted with His character, you will always know His will. This knowledge will produce a boldness and freedom from condemnation in your life.

We need to declare war on the condemnation that torments the lives of so many Christians. God's will is that we walk in His every promise, full of boldness, confidence and love. By bearing much fruit and receiving His promises, God is glorified. We need to understand this. It is not humility to refuse to accept what God has provided for us. Although it may appear to be an attitude of true humility, it is nothing more than pride, foolishness and false humility.

What the world calls pride is often what the Bible calls humility and boldness. Humility is simply submitting one's thoughts to God's way of thinking, while pride refuses to do so. It is one thing to refuse God's promises due to ignorance; but to refuse them even after the truth is revealed, is nothing but pride, in spite of how "humble" and meek it may appear.

Some of the proudest people can have an appearance of humility. But what counts is not our appearance, it is our attitude toward the Word of God. Jesus said, *He who has my commandments and keeps them, it is he who loves Me* (John 14:21). It is not enough just to talk about His commandments.

The Character of God is Revealed in Creation

Creation is a demonstration of God's character. God always creates and works in accordance with His nature. His surroundings are formed by His character and they reveal His nature.

Let's take a look now at what He has created.

Then God said, "Let the waters abound with an abundance of living creatures, and let birds fly above the earth across the face of the firmament of the heavens" (Gen 1:20).

Notice the word "abundance," and remember that God expresses His character in what He creates. He did not just create three or four fish. He created them in abundance. God always does things properly. If you stop to look at the world around you, both the microscopic world and the visible world, you will notice that there is ample quantity and abundance in every area.

There are millions of flowers which, remain unseen by man. A human authority or committee would not allow this, claiming, "Having lots of flowers that no one can see is wasteful. We need to do something about this. Let's put asphalt there instead and move all the flowers to the center of town." But this is not the way God is. He has the resources to afford abundance.

Ever since I was a child I have wanted to see the Himalayas. A few years ago, I was given the opportunity to visit Bangladesh and later Nepal. Nepal, Tibet and the Himalayas are known as the top of the world. While I was there, God said to me, "This is the best view of the world. Just look at the mountains!"

It was spectacular. I could not get enough of it—and when I left I still had a picture of those mountains in my mind. Something had happened. God had placed a permanent picture of that mountain range in my spirit, and since then, it has been much easier for me to think big.

If you are open to Him, God will use His creation to do something in you and for you. The Bible tells us that He speaks through His creation. Why do you think He created all those mountain ranges and peaks if not to challenge us to do the same—in the spirit? Why do you think He created such amazingly intricate flowers, some of which are virtually invisible? It's because He wants us to understand how concerned He is with the minute details in our lives.

Certain theologians say that it is wrong to think that God cares about the small, everyday occurrences in our lives. But our God does care. My God is the God of abundance who meets every one of my needs—both the little details and the big issues as well.

God demonstrates His nature and character in creation. He reveals that He is a God of abundance. He can afford to create things in abundance. He is not stingy with anything.

We read about creation in Genesis 1:31, *Then God saw everything that He had made, and indeed it was very good.* When God was finished, He put His stamp of approval on creation: "Made in heaven!"

God deposited gold and other precious metals in the mountains. He put reproductive ability in the earth and placed man over it, to tend it and put it to use. In doing all this He said, "It is good." The devil, on the other hand, tells us creation is evil. "Be careful!" he says, "it's dangerous!" But God called it good and accepted it. It is important that we too have this view of created, material things. They are not evil, bad or dangerous; they are good.

In Genesis 2:8 we read that God planted a garden. He planted the garden eastward in Eden and there He put the man whom He had formed. The name of the garden was *Eden*. In Hebrew this word means **riches, abundance** and **delight**. These were the surroundings in which God put man.

God Created Beauty

In other words, God placed Adam in the Garden of Eden, an environment of riches, abundance and delight. Genesis 2:9 says, *And out of the ground the Lord God made every tree grow that is pleasant to the sight and good for food.*

God has never considered beauty and good taste taboo. The devil has perverted these things. He has made people hedonistic and sensual, living only by their feelings and completely imprisoned by sensuality. As a result, Christians have responded in fear by rejecting anything that stimulates the five senses. They have difficulty permitting themselves to enjoy things and being afraid of becoming "worldly," they live stingy lives.

God wants you to be neither greedy nor to live only after your senses. However, He does not want you to dissociate yourself from what He has created.

There was a time in my early Christian life when I thought it was wrong to do just about everything. I believed that getting God to bless me was extremely hard, but I discovered that this is not at all the case. God created beautiful colors and beauty itself and therefore, He has nothing against you using them. God desires to encourage you and set you free in this area.

Freedom outside of Jesus Christ is a destructive force. We must not use our freedom to indulge in the flesh. But if you are filled with the Holy Spirit, love Jesus and have made Him your Lord, you have the right to enjoy and bless others, with all that God has given you. This was God's original intention for your life.

If your motives are pure and you have a longing to follow Christ Jesus, it is not difficult to part with things when prompted by God to do so. Your possessions do not own or bind you. God's intention was for you to eat of the trees that were good for food and pleasant to the sight. It's interesting to notice that one of the first things said about the garden is that the trees were pleasant to the sight.

God Has No Lack

Now a river went out of Eden to water the garden, and from there it parted and became four riverheads. The name of the first is Pishon; it is the one which encompasses the whole land of Havilah, where there is gold. And the gold of that land is good. Bdellium and the onyx stone are there (Gen 2:10-12 KJV).

God did not warn Adam and Eve about going to this land or tell them that they would fall into sin because of the gold and precious stones there. It was God who put these things in the earth and here, in this scripture, He is actually describing the site. He even says that the gold there was good.

Gold is good when used for the right things. It is not sinful in itself, otherwise God would not have created it. Heaven is full of gold. The temple in Jerusalem was bulging with it. It is the greed for gold that is sin—walking on others to get at it. Gold is not sinful, it is simply a precious metal! Metals are created by God and deposited in the earth so that we can discover them and use them to glorify Him.

When God viewed His creation prior to the Fall, He saw that it was good. By saying this, He meant that it was perfect and without deficiency. When God created the world and man, there was no such thing as poverty. Poverty is completely foreign to the nature of God, who is the God of abundance. He creates things in accordance with His own nature: pressed down, shaken together and running over.

Before the thief came poverty did not exist. When someone steals from you, you always become poorer and suffer loss. For this reason, Jesus calls the devil a thief. He steals, kills and destroys.

Poverty was non-existent before the Fall, but after the Fall came spiritual and physical death, sickness, shortage, loneliness, hatred, murder, poverty and so on. These entered the world as a direct result of sin. Poverty did not come from God. There was no poverty in the Garden of Eden, otherwise God would have called it poverty, deficiency and malnutrition. Instead, He put man in a garden of abundance, riches and delight.

Remember also, that there will be no deficiency in the new heavens and the new earth. God is the God of abundance in all that He does.

A Higher Level of Poverty

We must understand that there is a curse over the earth and over all of creation, and that if it were not for Jesus, we would have to wear ourselves out just to survive.

In 1982, when I returned to Sweden from America, where I had been attending Bible school, the first thing the devil told me was, "You can preach faith and healing here but not finances because people will think you are Americanized, so don't say anything about money!"

Just as I was about to accept this thought, I recognized where it came from. The Lord then spoke to me and said, "You need to preach prosperity in Sweden more than anything else."

I was amazed at this. Sweden is one of the most highly developed countries in the world. "Surely no one is poor in this country," I thought. But God showed me the people. He showed me how worn their clothing was and how they could hardly afford the basic necessities of life. God said, "Look at them! They are in need." He reminded me of the many people who are up to their ears in credit card bills. "Sweden is a poor country, although its poverty is on a much higher level than many other countries," He said.

The newspapers report about the large numbers of people in Sweden who live in poverty and want. The price of food is high, take-home pay has decreased and people are tied to their credit cards. They buy and borrow foolishly and end up in even greater bondage, under the heavy yoke of financial burden. Jesus wants to lift these burdens.

We all know that in the end times, the devil wants to make the whole world part of the same credit account and eventually, put that account number on their foreheads. We, on the other hand, will continue to teach about financial prosperity as we become increasingly dependant on "El Shaddai."

2

The Blessing of Abraham

There is abundance in heaven. Jesus prayed, *Your will be done on earth as it is in heaven* (Matt 6:10). Poverty is a curse on this earth that came because of mankind's fall into sin. This curse over the ground made it necessary for man to toil in the sweat of his brow, before it would produce. The earth no longer produced of itself.

After some time under these conditions, God chose a man named Abram (whose name God later changed to Abraham) and made a covenant with him:

> Now the Lord had said to Abram: "Get out of your country, from your family and from your father's house, to a land that I will show you. I will make you a great nation; I will bless you and make your name great; and you shall be a blessing. I will bless those who bless you, and I will curse him who curses you; and in you all the families of the earth shall be blessed." So Abram departed as the Lord had spoken to him (Gen 12:1-4).

The blessing God placed on this man is known as the blessing of Abraham. It was a blessing that would be available for all generations throughout all eternity. The scriptures tell us that we have received the blessing of Abraham, through Christ Jesus. We share in the same faith as Abraham and therefore we are his seed (see Gal 3:7).

God blessed Abraham and his seed. At one point in his life Abraham went to Egypt for a while. The

Bible tells us how God blessed him while he was there:

> Then Abram went up from Egypt, he and his wife and all that he had, and Lot with him, to the South. Abram was very rich in livestock, in silver and in gold.... Lot also, who went with Abram, had flocks and herds and tents (Gen 13:1-2,5).

Lot was rich because he stayed with Abraham. There are people today who are just like Lot. They stay close to where they can enjoy some of the blessings, but they have no faith of their own. When they leave those who are blessed, they lose their blessings.

You have been personally blessed by God. The place where you put your foot is blessed. The people you come in contact with are blessed. If you walk with God as Abraham did, the people around you will be blessed, whether they happen to like you or not.

Never Help Yourself!

> Now the land was not able to support them, that they might dwell together, for their possessions were so great that they could not dwell together. And there was strife between the herdsmen of Abram's livestock and the herdsmen of Lot's livestock. The Canaanites and the Perizzites then dwelt in the land. So Abram said to Lot, "Please let there be no strife between you and me, and between my herdsmen and your herdsmen; for we are brethren. Is not the whole land before you? Please separate from me. If you take the left, then I will go to the right; or if you go to the right, then I will go to the left." And Lot lifted his eyes and saw all the plain of Jordan, that it was well watered everywhere (before the Lord destroyed Sodom and Gomorrah) like the garden of the Lord, like the land

of Egypt as you go towards Zoar. Then Lot chose for himself all the plain of Jordan (Gen 13:6-11).

Abraham's herdsmen began to argue, but Abraham himself was of another spirit. He was blessed and knew the God he served. He refused to dispute with Lot about the land and even went so far as to give it to Lot. Those who walk with the God of abundance need never be greedy.

Lot's greed became apparent in this situation. He had been given the opportunity of a lifetime. He was just about to make a real killing. He was free to help himself and that is exactly what he did.

Never help yourself to something, whether it is a possession, a ministry or a position. Some preachers push their way around and are eager to receive invitations to speak. You never need draw attention to yourself. If you have something, it will be noticed. You need to be like Abraham and let others take the best. If God has promised you something, it will be yours, regardless.

Lot had no faith in God; so he reacted as he did and consequently lost everything. Jesus said in Matthew 16:25, *Whoever desires to save his life will lose it, and whoever loses his life for My sake will find it.*

Abraham was Rich

Abraham was extremely rich—in livestock, silver and gold. He was probably the wealthiest man in the Middle East at that time. But his riches did not prevent him from serving God; in fact, he was the only one who did serve God.

Genesis 14 relates an interesting account of an incident in Lot's life and in so doing, reveals

Abraham's character and also the blessing of God that was over his life. Lot, we are told, ran into problems and was captured and robbed of everything he owned. Both Lot and all his goods were taken by the enemy. Abraham, however, was not delighted to hear of Lot's misfortune.

Now when Abram heard that his brother was taken captive, he armed his three hundred and eighteen trained servants who were born in his own house, and went in pursuit as far as Dan (Gen 14:14). Abraham and his men defeated the enemy army and rescued Lot and all his family and possessions. Think what a victory this was. 318 men were able to put the enemy to flight.

Abraham had more than just 318 servants. These men were hand-picked from seven or eight hundred others. You may have imagined Abraham as an old man who wandered around alone in the desert, followed by his wife, Sarah, thinking they, pitched their little two-man tent and squeezed in together. But it was not at all like this. Abraham lived in a tent, but have you ever stopped to think what his tent looked like?

A nomad is often forced to move because of his large herds of cattle and livestock. A brick house is, therefore, not the most practical kind of dwelling for this mobile lifestyle. By understanding the culture of the nomadic people in this part of the world, we know that they lead their herds to oases and other places where pasture can be found. They cannot build palaces for themselves.

However, if you visit a bedouin tent even today, you will find thick layers of carpets that are worth thousands of dollars each. The tents are full of gold and treasure chests, but from the outside all you

see are the gray colored goat skins, which offer
protection from the heat of the sun.

The Blessing is Passed On

We need to realize that when the Bible says that
God blessed Abraham with oxen and other livestock,
it means that God blessed him financially. He blessed
and increased the work of his hands and made him
prosperous. God passed this blessing on to Abraham's
son Isaac.

> Then God said: "No, Sarah your wife shall bear you
> a son, and you shall call his name Isaac; I will establish
> My covenant with him for an everlasting covenant,
> and with his descendants after him" (Gen 17:19).

The covenant God made with Abraham was an
eternal covenant that applied both to Isaac and to
all his descendants. We as believers are also
partakers in this covenant.

Genesis 26:1-6 tells us about the blessings of God
that came to Isaac:

> There was a famine in the land, besides the first
> famine that was in the days of Abraham. And Isaac
> went to Abimelech king of the Philistines in Gerar.
> Then the Lord appeared to him and said: "Do not go
> down to Egypt; dwell in the land of which I shall tell
> you. Sojourn in this land, and I will be with you and
> bless you; for to you and your descendants I give all
> these lands, and I will perform the oath which I swore
> to Abraham your father. And I will make your
> descendants multiply as the stars of heaven; I will
> give to your descendants all these lands; and in your
> seed all the nations of the earth shall be blessed;
> because Abraham obeyed my voice and kept my charge,
> my commandments, my statutes, and my laws." So
> Isaac dwelt in Gerar. Isaac inherited his father's

camels, donkeys, silver, gold and his servants. When famine came, he naturally thought he should journey on to a better land. But instead God said, "No, Egypt is not to be your source. Egypt is not to provide food for your flocks or make you rich, I am the one who will do it. Stay in this land in spite of the famine. Trust in me and I will bless you. This is the land I will give to you."

So Isaac remained in the land and sowed his crops there. He sowed in a time of famine and because the Lord blessed him, he reaped a harvest of one hundredfold that year (see verse 12).

Obedience Leads to Influence

Isaac was immediately blessed when he obeyed what God had said. He was the only one in the country to receive such a harvest and it came as a direct result of the blessing of God over his life. In spite of the famine and the curse, with all of its many difficulties, God released His blessing over Isaac.

Genesis 26:13-14 says, *The man began to prosper, and continued prospering until he became very prosperous; for he had possessions of flocks and possessions of herds and a great number of servants. So the Philistines envied him.*

People had not paid much attention to the old man Abraham while he was still alive. But suddenly, his son came along and grew to be a mighty man. The Philistines became nervous as the ground beneath their feet began to crumble, because as Isaac walked he said, "I praise you, God, that this ground belongs to me. These people live here, but I own this land. I just thank you for your blessing!"

The same is true for us. God has said that the whole earth belongs to us and, like Isaac, we too can walk in the blessings of our God. Suddenly, we have become mighty and influential in the spirit realm, and in every other realm as well. The Church is beginning to grow up. It is no longer a prayer group of three or four people, but it has now become a true Church.

God's will is that we increase. He wants us to have such an influence on our surroundings, that His power and love and His revelation and Word affect people's lives.

The devil fights God's revelation at two points: first, as it comes to you and second, as you pass it on. The devil gets nervous when you become a channel for God, by blessing people with what God has given you.

We see an example of how the devil attempted to hinder the flow of God's blessings to Isaac in Genesis 26:15, when the Philistines tried to stop the water supply by filling the wells Abraham had dug.

Now the Philistines had stopped up all the wells which his father's servants had dug in the days of Abraham his father, and they had filled them with earth. By doing this they tried to stop Isaac's livestock from getting water, but we see in verse 18, that Isaac simply reopened the wells. There was a constant fight over the wells because of their importance in feeding the flocks and livestock.

The devil tries to block the flow of provision to us as God's people, so we become unable to accomplish all that God wants. Additionally, if we do not give tithes and offerings, then the devil has succeeded in preventing the necessary resources from reaching those who need it to do His work. This is where the battle lies. For this reason, we must be financially independent in the Lord and able to do and accomplish all that God desires.

Financial Blessing in the Covenant

The blessing of Abraham was passed on to Isaac and then from Isaac, to Jacob. In Genesis 27, Isaac blesses Jacob under the false belief that he is his son, Esau. Because a spoken blessing cannot be revoked, Jacob retained the blessing.

> And he came near and kissed him; and he smelled the smell of his clothing, and blessed him and said, "Surely, the smell of my son is like the smell of a field which the Lord has blessed. Therefore may God give you of the dew of heaven, of the fatness of the earth, and plenty of grain and wine. Let peoples serve you, and nations bow down to you. Be master over your brethren, and let your mother's sons bow down to you. Cursed be everyone who curses you, and blessed be those who bless you! (Gen 27:27-29).

This was the same blessing given by God to Abraham. He was blessed with the fatness and the fruit of the earth and with plenty of grain and wine; he was blessed in abundance.

> Then Jacob made a vow, saying, "If God will be with me, and keep me in this way that I am going, and give me bread to eat and clothing to put on, so that I come back to my father's house in peace, then the Lord shall be my God. And this stone which I have set as a pillar shall be God's house, and of all that you give me I will surely give a tenth to you" (Gen 28:20-21).

Here, we can see that the tithe was not originally a commandment of the law. It came before the Mosaic law was established and goes back as far as

Abraham and the days of Melchizedek the high priest (see Gen 14:18-20). The principle of the tithe existed before it became a part of the Law of Moses, just as it continues now that the law has been fulfilled.

God is Your Provider

Jacob was at odds with his older brother Esau, because he had tricked him out of the blessing. He departed with nothing and left Esau behind, with all that his father, Isaac, owned. He labored for many years to earn his wives and his keep at the home of Laban. But then God began to bless him, in spite of his faults, imperfections and many mistakes.

In Genesis 31:7-9, Jacob says to his wives, *Your father has deceived me and changed my wages ten times, but God did not allow him to hurt me. If he said thus: "The speckled shall be your wages," then all the flocks bore speckled. And if he said thus: "The streaked shall be your wages," then all the flocks bore streaked. So God has taken away the livestock of your father and given them to me.*

There is a principle to be remembered here: If you are blessed, which you are, you need never try to get something by force. If you are mistreated, you do not need to defend yourself. You will quickly realize that the more you serve God and fellowship with the Lord, and the more you affect the lives of others, the more people will try to misuse and exploit you. You need to learn this and decide in advance, not to become disappointed or angry with people, who only want to use you.

If you stay in close fellowship with the Lord, God will always turn these situations around for good. Like Joseph, you might be thrown into a well by your brothers, sold as a slave into Egypt and end up in prison. But, one day you will find yourself with Pharaoh's ring on your finger, if this is what God has planned.

Your life will be just as God has said if you keep to the vision He has promised, rather than becoming bitter, disappointed or irritated with people. Joseph is a wonderful example of a man who protected his heart from hate, envy, bitterness and disappointment toward those who had treated him wrongly.

Gold Belongs to the People of God

Now back in Genesis, we find that the time came when Jacob, full of fear, returned to meet Esau. Jacob had nothing when he left home. But when he came back again, he had so much that he was able to divide everything into two large companies of camels, donkeys and livestock and even give one away, in an attempt to bribe Esau and win his favor. But because Esau was already favorably disposed toward Jacob, he wanted no gifts. His possessions had prospered as well.

Perfection is not a requirement for the blessings of God. What really matters is the person's heart attitude. If the heart is right, the blessings of God will immediately begin to flow.

The blessing received by Abraham was passed to his son Isaac, then to Jacob and eventually, to the whole nation of Israel. This was the blessing of Abraham. We know about the misery that Israel later experienced in Egypt; but we also know that

God delivered them. *He also brought them out with silver and gold, and there was none feeble among his tribes* (Ps 105:37).

The word "feeble" means infirm or sick. Infirmity and sickness are the same thing. No one was sick among the tribes of Israel when they came out of Egypt. God had healed every one of them who had eaten of the Passover lamb. This was a pattern of Jesus Christ, the spotless lamb of God, who died and took on Himself our sickness and disease; ...*by whose stripes you were healed.*

However, healing and the forgiveness of sins are not the only promises included in redemption. We read that God brought His people out of Egypt with silver and gold. The Egyptians finally gave the Israelites their silver and gold, just to get them to leave the country and put an end to the plagues. Egypt was under an extreme curse for a short period of its history. The Egyptians clearly saw the difference between who was blessed and who was not. By giving their gold to Israel, they exemplified the fact that the wealth of the sinners is stored up for the righteous (Prov 13:22).

This gold was later used to build the tabernacle in the desert, through the freewill offerings of the people. Something was built with the gold God brought to His people. The same principle applies today.

Don't Forget the Source of Wealth!

And it shall be, when the Lord your God brings you into the land of which he swore to your fathers, to Abraham, Isaac, and Jacob, to give you large and beautiful cities which you did not build, houses full of all good things, which you did not fill, hewn-out wells which you did not dig, vineyards and olive trees which you did not plant—when you have eaten and are full—then beware, lest you forget the Lord who brought you out of the land of Egypt, from the house of bondage. You shall fear the Lord your God and serve him, and shall take oaths in His name (Deut 6:10-13).

The children of Israel lived in lack, famine, slavery and bondage in the land of Egypt. They were not allowed to worship their God, but then God delivered them. He brought them into a land where they had all they needed in every area of their lives; a land in which God met their needs in abundance.

Nowhere in the Old Testament does God warn the children of Israel about becoming rich. He warns them only about forgetting the One who gave them their riches.

In Deuteronomy 8:4, the Lord reminds His people that their clothing did not wear out nor did their feet swell, for forty years. God supernaturally looked after their clothing. He provided for them miraculously, while they were in the wilderness and unable to weave or spin clothes for themselves. But this was not God's perfect will He did not want them to have to spend forty years in the desert. Elijah proved that the same distance could be traveled in only forty days when he walked from Israel down to Horeb (1 Kings 19:8).

The children of Israel wandered in the wilderness for forty years, because of their rebellion. In spite of this, the Lord was still their provider. He provided them with food from heaven, led them to springs and prevented their clothes from wearing out. However, his perfect will for them was that they live an abundant life in the promised land where there would be a continuously rich harvest from whatever they sowed. This is a picture of abundant life.

> When you have eaten and are full, and have built beautiful houses and dwell in them; and when your herds and your flocks multiply, and your silver and your gold are multiplied, and all that you have is multiplied; when your heart is lifted up, and you forget the Lord your God who brought you out of the land of Egypt, from the house of bondage; who led you through that great and terrible wilderness, in which were fiery serpents and scorpions and thirsty land where there was no water; who brought water for you out of the rock of flint; who fed you in the wilderness with manna, which your fathers did not know, that he might humble you and that he might test you, to do you good in the end—then you say in your heart, "My power and the might of my hand have gained me this wealth." And you shall remember the Lord your God, for it is he who gives you power to get wealth, that he may establish His covenant which he swore to your fathers, as it is this day (Deut 8:12-18).

This means that the eternal covenant made with Abraham and his seed, Isaac, Jacob and Israel, included the power to get wealth. When you gain this wealth, which you will do, because God has promised by oath to keep the covenant, you are not to forget that He is your source.

The Bible does not say that the poorer you are, the more humble you are, and the better you can serve and glorify God. No, it says that when you walk according to the covenant, God will bless you even in the financial area of your life. God will be glorified when you give Him the credit for this, but if you fail to do so, nothing will work for you.

Wealth—A Mark of Royalty

Romans 5:17 tells us that we have been made to reign in life, through Jesus Christ. We are kings and priests and God has made us a chosen, royal priesthood (see 1 Pet 2:9). Like David, a king is one who rules and reigns and exercises power. However, David was also characterized as a king by His prosperity. We read about this in First Chronicles 29:2-3:

> Now for the house of my God I have prepared with all my might: gold for things to be made of gold, silver for things of silver, bronze for things of bronze, iron for things of iron, wood for things of wood, onyx stones, stones to be set, stones, and marble slabs in abundance. Moreover, because I have set my affection on the house of my God, I have given to the house of my God, over and above all that I have prepared for the holy house, *my own special treasure* of gold and silver.

Here we can clearly see that as a king, David walked in royal authority and prosperity. He gave to the construction of the temple from the abundance of his own silver and gold. He even distinguished between his own personal possessions and that which was designated for building the temple.

David was a king on all levels. He was a king in terms of his dignity, in terms of his relationship with the Lord and in terms of his financial prosperity. We are also kings and priests to the Lord. We give what we have, and by putting it all at the Lord's disposal, He can do whatever He wants with it.

Blessings

We know that we have been blessed with the blessing of Abraham because, according to Galatians 3:13-14, Jesus Christ has become a curse for us so that this blessing could come to the Gentiles, and so we could receive the promise of the Spirit. We receive the Spirit in order to receive abundant life. Through the Holy Spirit, the Body of Christ is able to partake in the blessings of the New Covenant, which also includes the blessing of Abraham.

We read about this blessing of Abraham in further detail in Deuteronomy 28. If you follow God and walk in obedience, if you are committed to Him and love Him above all else, then all of the blessings mentioned in this chapter will come to you, as long as you do not refuse to accept them. Of course, you will not receive them if you do not believe that they are there for you.

But, *if you diligently obey the voice of the Lord your God, to observe carefully all His commandments...the Lord your God will set you high above all the nations of the earth. And all these blessings shall come upon you and overtake you* (Deut 28:1-2).

In Hebrew the word "overtake" carries the implication that something you cannot avoid is thrown at you, similar to a heat-seeking missile! It continues to pursue until it has reached its target.

What then follows in Deuteronomy 28 is a lengthy list of blessings that will come over you: *Blessed shall you be in the city,* verses 3-4 declare, *and blessed shall you be in the country. Blessed shall be the fruit of your body, the produce of your ground and the increase of your herds, the increase of your cattle and the offspring of your flocks.* All this is concerned with your work, your livelihood. The things the Bible mentions here were the primary sources of income at that time.

Ephesians 4:28 says, *Let him who stole steal no longer, but rather let him labor, working with his hands what is good, that he may have something to give him who has need.*

If you are constantly working but receiving only enough to make ends meet, you have nothing to share with those who are in need. Your work should be so blessed that you have an abundance from which you can give to every good work.

Deuteronomy 28:5 says, *Blessed shall be your basket and your kneading bowl.* This applies to your food.

Verses 6-7 tell us, *Blessed shall you be when you come in, and blessed shall you be when you go out. The Lord will cause your enemies who rise against you to be defeated before your face; they shall come out against you one way and flee before you seven ways.* In these scriptures, God is promising victory over the attacks in your life; the times when the devil comes to steal, kill and destroy and take what God has given you. But He who is in you, is greater than he who is in the world (1 John 4:4).

We find in verses 8-9 that, *The Lord will command the blessing on you in your storehouses* (in your cupboards; your larder and freezer) *and in all that you set your hand, and he will bless you in the land which the Lord your God is giving you. The Lord will establish you as a holy people to Himself, just as He has sworn to you, if you keep the commandments of the Lord your God and walk in His ways.*

Continuing in verse 11, the Bible tells us, *And the Lord will grant you plenty of goods.* John 16:24 says, *Until now, you have asked nothing in My name.*

Ask, and you will receive, that your joy may be full. God wants your joy to be complete in Him.

In fact, in Deuteronomy 28:11-12, He says He will give you plenty, *in the fruit of your body, in the increase of your livestock, and in the produce of your ground, in the land of which the Lord swore to your fathers to give you. The Lord will open to you His good treasure, the heavens, to give the rain to your land in its season, and to bless all the work of your hand. You shall lend to many nations, but you shall not borrow.* Although you may not yet be at this point, this is your ultimate goal.

Curses

We have just seen that the blessings of God apply to every area of your life—your family, your finances and your health. Every aspect of your life will be blessed *if* you hear the voice of the Lord your God. However, if you fail to hear His voice, you will come under a curse. The Lord knows that the curse, which is in the world will come over us, if we choose to disobey, by following our own ways and the ways of the world. Therefore, we are continually encouraged and commanded to walk in obedience to Him.

In Deuteronomy 28, beside the list of blessings we may enjoy, there is also a long list of the various types of curses that disobedience brings. We will name just a few of them.

Verse 29 mentions that there will be plundering. Verse 30 says, *you shall plant a vineyard, but shall not gather its grapes.* This is what it means to be in lack.

We find in verse 33 that, *A nation whom you have not known shall eat the fruit of your land and the produce of your labor.* To work hard without achieving results is a curse.

Verse 38 goes on to say, *You shall carry much seed out to the field and gather but little in.* This means that you will have nothing left over to put in storage.

In verse 42 we read, *Locusts shall consume all your trees and the produce of your land.*

Previous roles are reversed as verse 44 states that the alien shall lend to you, but you shall not lend to him.

Verse 48 says, *you shall serve your enemies, whom the Lord will send against you, in hunger, in thirst, in nakedness, and in need of all things; and he will put a yoke of iron on your neck until he has destroyed you.* This was the situation the people had in Egypt.

Even for you today, when you leave the blessings of God, the curses of "Egypt" will come over you once again and you will find yourself in need of all things. This is not the will of God, but, *Because you did not serve the Lord your God joyfully and gladly in the time of prosperity* (Deut 28:47 NIV), it will come on you.

Be Thankful!

God's will is that you live in prosperity and serve Him with joy and gladness of heart. The first tendency toward sin is ungratefulness. For this reason you should be sure to thank God for all that He has given you, without complaining or grumbling. It is important that you praise the Lord for what He gives you, because it was through ingratitude that man fell into sin.

If you maintain joy, gratitude and a right attitude—in spite of how the circumstances may look—God will bless you in increasing measure.

You will even be able to enjoy these blessings without becoming materialistic. They will be a blessing to you and to others, and God will be able to use you effectively when it comes to sharing with those in need and in financing the Gospel. You will be a blessing and through this, God will be glorified.

3

Righteousness— The prerequisite

According to the Word of God, if you have received Jesus Christ as your Savior, then you have been made righteous. Wherever the Word of God refers to the righteous, it is referring to you. Never forget that you have been made righteous and that every promise given to those who are righteous, has been given to you through Christ Jesus.

The righteous are not those who behave well, they are those who have had their sins forgiven. Righteousness is a position that you have received, based on the work of Jesus Christ. It is completely independent of your feelings. You cannot become more or less righteous. You have been made righteous once and for all.

You are a child of God even when you happen to be disobedient, although, until you ask for forgiveness, disobedience will prevent righteousness from reigning in your life. David said, *Blessed is he whose transgression is forgiven* (Ps 32:1). Righteousness is a legal position—not an emotional feeling.

Blessed is the man, the Bible declares, *who fears the Lord, Who delights greatly in His commandments* (Ps 112:1). This obedience comes through faith, and involves listening intently to what God has to say and then, being willing to do it. The devil does all he can to stop you from entering into this obedience.

But the Bible clearly shows us that obedience to the Word of God releases blessing in our lives.

Second Corinthians 10:5 speaks of strongholds that raise up against the knowledge of God, which must first be pulled down before obedience can come. When active obedience is established, the blessings will begin to enter your life.

The Fear of God Brings Wealth

Blessed is the man who fears the Lord, Who delights greatly in His commandments. His descendants will be mighty on earth; The generation of the upright will be blessed. Wealth and riches will be in his house, And his righteousness endures for ever. Unto the upright there arises light in the darkness; He is gracious, and full of compassion, and righteousness. A good man deals graciously and lends; He will guide his affairs with discretion (Ps 112:1-5).

The Bible goes on to say in verse 7 that the righteous, *will not be afraid of evil tidings.* Because you are righteous, when your circumstances directly contradict what God says, your heart can remain steadfast and established.

Verse 8 says about the righteous that, *His heart is established; he will not be afraid.* His soul and spirit are established and steadfast. Isaiah 26:3 says that God will keep in perfect peace those whose minds are stayed on Him. Peace and blessing come as a result of a steadfast heart and mind. In other words, if you are aware of what God has said and have decided to agree with it and apply it to your life, your mind will stop constantly swinging back and forth like a pendulum.

He has dispersed abroad, verse 9 tells us, *he has given to the poor; his righteousness endures forever.*

When the righteous delight greatly in the commandments of God and fear the Lord, wealth and riches will be in their house (see verses 1-3).

This means that wealth and riches in your house are a direct blessing from the Lord because you fear Him and keep His commandments. It is your legal right because it is promised in the scriptures and because you are one who is righteous and fears God and obeys His commands. Wealth and riches are a blessing from the Lord. The Bible calls them blessings, not curses.

We have already seen from the Word of God that there are blessings and there are curses; and that one of the curses is poverty. Poverty is a curse and does not come from God, but entered the world as a result of man's sin and rebellion. Whether clothed in secular or religious garments, poverty has one aim—to rob people of the blessings of God and to prevent them from doing what He has called them to do.

Psalm 35:27 says that the Lord has pleasure in the prosperity of His servants. We must destroy the opposition to this truth which, is caused by envy, stinginess and poverty. Being clothed in rags is not a virtue, nor is it pleasing to God. He delights in the prosperity of His servants. However, God does not delight in greed.

The Bible says, *Every plant which My heavenly Father has not planted will be uprooted* (Matt 15:13). Greediness and poverty thinking are plants that have been cultivated for centuries and have influenced you more than you can imagine. Many times you have wanted to please others by appearing unassuming or modest. However, it is much more important to please God, who says that He has pleasure in the prosperity of His servants. Your correct response should be to let God be pleased by your prosperity. When you have the revelation of this, you will have no more problems in this area.

Wisdom Brings Riches

God said to King Solomon, *Ask! What shall I give you?* (1 Kings 3:5). Solomon did not ask God for might or riches, instead he asked for wisdom. God granted him riches and honor along with wisdom, because he had requested what was on the Lord's heart.

If you seek the Kingdom of God, all other things will be added to you (see Matt 6:33). Your attitude is all important. You seek first the Kingdom of God, by seeking Christ Jesus and His Word. You need to know what God's Word has to say in the area of finances. You must see the Kingdom of God established in this area of your life, so that you can walk in faith with a good conscience.

If you honor God with your possessions and are constantly looking for opportunities to give things away, *your barns will be filled with plenty, and your vats will overflow with new wine* (see Prov 3:9-10). This is a picture of abundant life. God has promised to prosper you when you make your possessions available to Him. Prosperity is a direct result of your obedience in this area.

Isaiah 1:19 says, *If you are willing and obedient, you shall eat the good of the land*. Willingness and obedience produce blessing. You have been given a free will and the ability to choose. God wants obedience to operate in your life, bringing with it His blessing.

Proverbs 10:22 says that the blessing of the Lord makes one rich and He adds no sorrow with it. God does not include a small amount of sorrow in His blessings, to test you. When God blesses you in the area of finances, He will protect His blessing so that it does not cause you any problems. He has determined that you will eat of the good of the land. He has made up His mind, and now it is up to you to enter the land, through obedience.

4

Riches in the Book of Proverbs

The book of Proverbs can be likened to a gold mine in which you can find valuable truths, especially in the area of financial prosperity.

Proverbs 3:9 says, *Honor the Lord with your possessions.* The prerequisite for all financial blessing is serving God. You never need to seek riches, for when you seek God, they will find you. The Bible tells us to seek first the Kingdom of God and all these things will be added to us (Matt 6:33).

Proverbs 3:12-13, describing the correction and the wisdom of the Lord, declares, *Happy is the man who finds wisdom.* Wisdom is supreme and it is this that God wants you to seek. The Bible never says, "Seek after gold and diamonds!" Instead it says, *If you seek her* (wisdom) *as silver, And search for her as for hidden treasures...* (Prov 2:4). And again, *For her proceeds are better than the profits of silver, And her gain than fine gold* (Prov 3:14).

What is this wisdom? It is Jesus Christ who has been made wisdom and understanding to us (see 1 Cor 1:30). Seek Jesus and His wisdom and understanding and when you have found Him you will be blessed and happy. You will profit more by wisdom, or the Word of God, than you will from silver and gold.

What are your priorities? How highly do you value the Word of God? If you secretly believe that the Bible is good but that a different set of criteria apply out in the real world, you have missed the point entirely. The Word of God is reality itself, for, *the reality...is found in Christ* (Col 2:17 NIV).

Proverbs 3:15-16 says, *She* (wisdom, or the Word) *is more precious than rubies, And all the things you may desire cannot compare with her. Length of days is in her right hand, In her left hand riches and honor.* This means that if you gain wisdom instead of silver, wisdom will in turn gain riches and honor for you.

We are told in Proverbs 3:33 that, *The curse of the Lord is on the house of the wicked, But He blesses the habitation of the just.* The Lord blesses both the house itself and that which is in it.

Proverbs 8:17-18 states, *I love those who love me, And those who seek me diligently will find me. Riches and honor are with me, Enduring riches and righteousness.*

Continuing to read in Proverbs 8, God's Word says, *I traverse the way of righteousness, In the midst of the paths of justice, That I may cause those who love me to inherit wealth, That I may fill their treasuries* (vv. 20-21).

This is still wisdom speaking here. Reliable Old Testament expositors agree that the wisdom Proverbs 8 describes is referring to Jesus, Himself. So it is actually Jesus speaking here. He is the One who traverses the way of righteousness and the paths of justice.

The phrase, "to inherit wealth," is not limited just to "spiritual" wealth. This inheritance is intended to fill your treasuries.

Paul said, *For we are not writing any other things to you than what you read or understand* (2 Cor

1:13). So when we read the scripture Which says, *I traverse the way of righteousness, In the midst of the paths of justice, That I may cause those who love me to inherit wealth,* we know that it contains nothing other than what we are able to read and understand.

You may think that this is too good to be true. That is not your problem. You might ask, "But how will it happen?" That is not your problem either. Say only, "Jesus, I praise you that your Words are true. I don't know how or when it will happen, all I know is what you have said. Let it be just as you have spoken."

Work and Wealth

Proverbs 10:4 says, *Lazy hands make a man poor* (NIV). This is also one of God's promises. It tells you exactly what to do if you want to become poor. Be lazy, inattentive and undisciplined and you will suffer lack, financially and in every other area of your life, as well. According to the covenant in Deuteronomy 28, God has given you the power to gain wealth. You are the one who gains the wealth, and you do it by working with diligent hands.

Diligent hands will bring you success in every area of your life. You must diligently claim the things that God has for you because God has given you the power to do so. Indeed, He expects you to actively work to obtain them, rather than simply expect them to fall out of heaven on top of you. Verse 4 ends by saying, *...but diligent hands bring wealth.*

We are told in Proverbs 10:15 that, *The rich man's wealth is his strong city; The destruction of the poor is their poverty*. Poverty is obviously destructive and not a blessing.

The blessing of the Lord makes one rich, And He adds no sorrow with it (Prov 10:22). You must work, but it will not result in blessing if you are completely reliant on your own strength. Even in your work you must rely on the Lord.

Proverbs 11:18 says, *The wicked man earns deceptive wages* (NIV). Though people may make their way in this world and achieve success for a time, without the blessing of the Lord they will not endure. However, he *who sows righteousness reaps a sure reward*. This is a good verse for preachers: when you sow righteousness, by preaching the Word of God, you will receive a sure reward.

As a preacher, it is important that you put your trust in God alone and do not put pressure on other ministers or their treasurers. When you sow righteousness you will receive a sure reward. You should not be dependent on other people's money. This is extremely important.

You do not need to beg or threaten, you only need to believe God. He is the source of your provision and, even if the church happens to be stingy, He has other channels. The key is that you obey what God says and continue to sow righteousness. In this way you honor God with your possessions.

The Work of God can be Hindered

Proverbs 11:23-24 says, *The desire of the righteous is only good, But the expectation of the wicked is wrath. There is one who scatters, yet increases more; And there is one who withholds more than is right,*

But it leads to poverty. These are the divine economical principles.

The generous soul will be made rich, And he who waters will also be watered himself. The people will curse him who withholds grain, But blessing will be on the head of him who sells it (vv. 25-26).

Among other things, withholding grain means refusing to give. As you know, Paul refers to money as seed. If God is directing a project intended to bless thousands of people and you withhold your "seed," many people will be cursed, including yourself.

In certain churches, there are servants of God whose visions remain unfulfilled due to rebellious people, who have destroyed the possibility of these visions becoming reality, by refusing to give financially. This is tragic, especially for those who refuse to give. Thousands of people fail to hear the message of the Gospel and are cursed as a result.

The key to this issue is consistent giving. Those who constantly save become only poorer, while those who give become wealthier. They give freely yet gain even more. This is the attitude you need: "I will not cling to my last penny but will give the last thing I have. Even if I should die, I will die a giver." However, a giver will not die.

Proverbs 11:31 says, *If the righteous receive their due on earth, how much more the ungodly and the sinner!* (NIV). We have often emphasized the fact that the ungodly receive their due here on earth while the righteous receive theirs in heaven. But that is not what this verse says. We do indeed receive a reward in heaven, but we will also receive a reward on earth. There are tremendous blessings waiting for us in heaven, just as there is a reward for us here, on earth.

Proverbs 13:11 states that, *Wealth gained by dishonesty will be diminished, But he who gathers by labor will increase. Poverty and shame will come to him who disdains correction, But he who regards reproof will be honored* (Prov 13:18). We see here again that obedience brings blessing.

Proverbs 13:22 says, *A good man leaves an inheritance to his children's children, But the wealth of the sinner is stored up for the righteous.* When the good, or righteous man dies he leaves an inheritance, not only for his children, but for his grandchildren as well. Having many grandchildren is a blessing from the Lord, however, your children have a right to your inheritance, so they need to have enough, before your grandchildren receive anything. In other words, your inheritance needs to be rather large to go around to both your children and your grandchildren.

The wealth of the sinner is stored up for the righteous. What does this mean? When the sinner dies, the possessions he has left behind are transferred into the Kingdom of God. God has the ability to cause the possessions that the ungodly man has greedily gathered up to be added to His Kingdom and distributed throughout the world, for the sake of the Gospel.

How does God bless financially? He does not have a mint in heaven, nor do bills usually fall from heaven. No, He channels the money that is already here on earth. Wealthy people, who are not saved, are reservoirs for the devil. They pile up possessions and gather wealth to themselves, thus restricting resources that could be put to much better, active use.

If you take this scripture seriously and begin to pray in accordance with it, you will release the contents of these reservoirs and cause them to be transferred to the righteous. Who needs money more than the righteous? Who needs earthly possessions more than the righteous?

We have been called to preach the Gospel to the world. We have been called to give to the poor. We have been called to bless others and expand the Kingdom of God. None of this is possible without money.

Abundance is More Than Enough

Proverbs 14:24 says, *The crown of the wise is their riches, But the foolishness of fools is folly*. What does a crown symbolize? It symbolizes **authority** and **honor**. Placing a crown on someone's head honors, blesses, and exalts that person. God is saying here that riches are a means by which the wise are honored. God's way of blessing and honoring the wise and the righteous is by giving them riches.

The word "riches" produces a certain emotional reaction. You may have been given the impression during your childhood that wealth was dangerous, negative and dirty. But the blessings of God are never dirty, they are only good. Only good things come from God. Being blessed by God is something good, not something bad which makes you feel ashamed. You need to begin to view riches in a way that is not worldly or religious.

Riches are synonymous with prosperity. Worldly thinking, though, makes riches synonymous with words like "greed," "excess" and "gluttony." This makes you either afraid of riches or too intimidated to ask God for anything associated with it. However, if you never ask for prosperity you will never receive it and unless you do, the financial resources of God, that are needed to carry out His work, will not be released.

You must see prosperity in the proper perspective. It is nothing more than **having your needs met in such a way that you have enough to give to others.** This is true prosperity and riches.

It is possible to be rich in a number of different ways. You can be rich in money, time, love and faith. Being rich means having so much of something that some of it can be distributed to others, without you, yourself, being in need. This is true prosperity, our goal.

It does not mean that your bedroom will be filled with bars of gold. This is not a goal in itself. You need to get rid of any delusions you may have regarding prosperity and discover what God actually means. Otherwise, you will have an unrealistic perspective about the subject and either end up daydreaming and fantasizing about being rich, or just feeling guilty every time money is mentioned.

The truth is that God gives you more than enough so that you can abundantly meet the needs of others.

You cannot only be rich in different ways, you can also be rich on a number of different levels, depending on what you are called to do. I do not believe that every believer is to be a multi-millionaire, although I do believe that God wants multi-millionaires, and that He can raise up such people who are supernatural givers. Each of us is a giver, but not all of us have the ministry of giving (see Rom 12:8).

Proverbs 15:6 says, *In the house of the righteous there is much treasure, But the revenue of the wicked is trouble*. The ungodly wear themselves out to get rich and their greed is under a curse, while the house of the righteous is full of treasure. This would imply that, as a righteous person, your house is allowed to contain furniture made of something other than rough wooden boards. You should not feel guilty about owning beautiful furniture.

Work and Wisdom

Now let's read in Proverbs 21:20: *There is desirable treasure, And oil in the dwelling of the wise, But a foolish man squanders it*. This scripture tells us that God is willing to bless your private life so that you have more than enough to meet your own needs. You are a blessing, not a curse.

A fool who becomes rich overnight cannot help letting his money go to his head. Not knowing what to do with it all, he quickly wastes everything. But the wise man is different. He increases his capital and receives supernatural wisdom and guidance on how he is to invest it, preserve it and cause it to increase.

Jesus spoke about this in the parable of the talents (see Matt 25:14-30). The servants who did the will of God caused their talent to yield interest and increase in value. This parable is taken directly from the world of banking. It tells us that we are not to be stingy or greedy; nor are we to throw or give away everything out of religious duty. Many have done just this.

Giving away everything is not a general principle. It is foolish for you to get yourself into a position where you are unable to support yourself and then expect others to pity you because of your stupidity. However, if God has told you to give away something, you will be blessed by doing so.

I have personally given things away and have been richly blessed as a result. At other times the Lord has told me not to give and the reason for this has later become apparent. You need to be sensitive and follow the Holy Spirit.

Proverbs 21:26 reads, *He covets greedily all day long, But the righteous gives and does not spare*. In other words, the righteous person does not save selfishly but is always ready to give. A covetous man is always greedy, whether or not he has something. You do not need to be rich to be greedy. Greed has nothing to do with riches, it is an attitude that can be shared by both poor and rich alike. Envy can be apparent in the rich man as well as in the man with nothing.

If you have a problem with this attitude, God wants to set you free. Envy has no place in the righteous man who is a consistent giver and has no need to spare or withhold. The righteous man always has plenty to give.

Proverbs 22:4 says, *Humility and the fear of the Lord bring wealth and honor and life* (NIV). If you maintain an attitude of humility, avoid proud and selfish thinking, and walk in the fear of the Lord, wealth, honor and life will come to you, as a result.

Proverbs 28:19-20 tells us, *He who tills his land will have plenty of bread, But he who follows frivolity will have poverty enough! A faithful man will abound with blessings, But he who hastens to be rich will not go unpunished.* The Word of God contains a built-in guillotine; it will not work for you unless your motives are correct.

You Can Demand Sevenfold in Return

People do not despise a thief, Proverbs 6:30-31 states, *If he steals to satisfy himself when he is starving. Yet when he is found, he must restore sevenfold; He may have to give up all the substance of his house.*

While this is meant to be a warning not to steal or covet, it also acts as a picture of the devil, who is the thief. When the devil steals something, he is to be forced to restore sevenfold. Bombard him with this verse when you find that he has stolen from you. Say to him:

"Satan, you have stolen from me and in the Name of Jesus I command you to restore sevenfold.

I thank you, Father, that your Word is true and that the thief will be punished. Father, I praise you that this promise is for me and I expect a sevenfold return on what the thief has taken."

You will experience attacks in this life, through which you will learn to walk in boldness, strength and protection. Proverbs 22:3 says that the wise man foresees evil and hides himself, but that the simple keep on going and suffer for it. This is why you must know the leading of the Holy Spirit in your life.

In certain situations, the Holy Spirit will exhort you to take a particular action, but at other times, He will warn you and try to calm you. If you are in too much of a hurry to sit down and think through the situation carefully, you will end up suffering for it.

You have undoubtedly, at some time or other done something foolish, that you know you should not have done. You probably felt all along that it was wrong, but you did it anyway and were stolen from as a result.

When this happens the first thing you need to do is to ask for forgiveness for failing to listen to the voice of God. You can then demand a sevenfold return of what Satan has stolen from you. However, this is only possible, when you have humbled yourself and admitted your wrongdoing. God gives life and riches to the humble. Romans 10:12 says, *He generously bestows His riches upon all who call upon Him* (AMP). God sees your heart and rewards you accordingly.

The Word of God is true. It applies to you and is valid right here and now. You do not ever need to be ashamed of His Word. If you have made a mistake, confess it as sin. Do not be ashamed of the blessings of God but expect them. If your heart is pure you can anticipate His blessings—God Himself has promised it!

5

Start Right Where You Are!

Will a man rob God? Yet you have robbed Me! But you say, 'In what way have we robbed You?' In tithes and offerings. You are cursed with a curse, for you have robbed Me, Even this whole nation. Bring all the tithes into the storehouse, That there may be food in My house, and try Me now in this," says the Lord of hosts, "If I will not open for you the windows of heaven and pour out for you such blessing That there will not be room enough to receive it" (Mal 3:8-10).

This is the only verse in the Bible that gives you the right to put God to the test. When you give, you have put yourself in a position to test Him by praying:

"I praise you, God, that your Word is true. I have now done what you have told me to do. I thank you that you will open the windows of heaven and pour out over me the blessings you have promised; such blessing that I do not have room for it all and have to give some of it away."

When your faith begins to operate in this area, you will do things you never dared to try before. However, God does not want you to suddenly run off and buy tickets to the Bahamas "in faith." Some people believe, for example, that it is all right to write a check hoping that the money to cover it will come in time. We are not talking about such foolishness. We are talking about God's desire for you to trust Him, rather than your circumstances, whether they are negative or positive.

The preaching of the Gospel in the power of the Holy Spirit is blessed. By doing so, you will become a soldier in the army of God. A soldier never worries about where to get his uniform, weapons and ammunition or where to find food and shelter. He simply expects these things to be provided for him and it is another person's responsibility to see that they are. The same is true for us; we do what we believe God has told us to do, even if we do not have the finances immediately available.

Prosperity is More Than Money

You need to understand that although God can bless you with a house and car, you cannot expect to start on that level. Riches has nothing to do with being a millionaire. There is a difference between this and prosperity. You must begin where you are. Just as in every other area of your life, you will learn to grow in prosperity.

Most people want everything instantaneously, but it does not work like this. This thinking is often just laziness; and, as we read before, only diligent hands will prosper. Neither will prosperity work if there is a motive of selfishness. But where there is a right attitude and an understanding of the Biblical principles of increase, prosperity will work.

You need to begin where you are, right now. It is all too easy to look at where others are and think to yourself, "I want to be there too." But how did they get there? What we are talking about here is true for every area: anointing, faith, financial prosperity, and so on. You want to get there overnight, while others have done it one step at a time. You cannot jump straight to the top. You must begin with the first step like they did.

God will bless you one step at a time. You need to believe this and refuse to be ashamed when you have to stand in faith for your needs, even if it is just for a pair of socks.

When the Lord first began to speak to me about financial prosperity, the only thing my wife and I had were stat loans. I noticed a house for sale in the newspaper one day and began to make some calculations in the margin. Our only resources were student loans, housing supplements and child benefit. Such a purchase was humanly impossible.

However, I felt an inner peace and God said to me, "You can do it if you really want to. Scrape together what you have and use it to pay your fixed bills and believe for your food, clothing and other needs." We had just enough to pay our monthly bills.

Sooner or later you have to make up your mind not to base financial decisions on how much money you presently have. If you want to get somewhere with God, you need to reach beyond your present financial limitations. However, unless you have a witness in your spirit this would be just foolishness. Nevertheless, if you are convinced that God has given you His approval to do something, you should step out and do it even if it appears that you do not have enough to begin with.

Personally speaking, ever since I began to walk in faith in this area, I have never seemed to have enough in the natural. My expenses are considerably larger than my income. But praise the Lord, He has always found a way to solve the problem. I do not walk by what I see; I walk by what God says.

If you have followed the Lord and given with a right heart, God will always meet your needs. But, it is not easy when you first begin to live this way. You may see no immediate results and feel the devil constantly harassing you, to make you stingy. But when the breakthrough finally comes, these principles will continue to operate throughout the rest of your life, as long as you continue to walk in faith, sow out to others, and guard this area.

PART II

FINANCIAL PROSPERITY IN THE NEW TESTAMENT

6

Jesus—Example and Substitute

Let's look now at what the New Testament has to say about money. We will begin by looking at Jesus Himself. Many people have an extremely peculiar picture of Him. They say, "We must not speak about money. Remember how Jesus walked around barefoot in Galilee. We should be just like Him." We should indeed be just like Jesus. He should be our example and our life should be patterned after His.

However, Jesus did some things specifically so that we would not have to do them. We need to keep in mind two areas when we consider the life of Jesus: first, His walk on earth and second, His work on the cross. In the first case He is our example and in the second case He is our substitute. We must properly appreciate both of these aspects of Jesus' life.

> Now it came to pass, afterwards, that He went through every city and village, preaching and bringing the glad tidings of the kingdom of God. And the twelve were with Him, and certain women who had been healed of evil spirits and infirmities—Mary called Magdalene, out of whom had come seven demons, and Joanna the wife of Chuza, Herod's steward, and Susanna, and *many others who provided for Him from their substance* (Luke 8:1-3).

The Correct Picture of Jesus

The devil has presented an extremely religious picture of Jesus. He was much more "normal" than we have believed. He was supernaturally normal. As a man, Jesus did all the things normally done by man. He experienced the same things as other human beings and, **like other men and women, Jesus also owned things.** The Bible even tells us that He lived in a house in Capernaum.

Jesus had a "traveling" ministry and so He did not spend His time sitting at home, in Capernaum. He often stayed with friends for as long as He was in a particular place.

Jesus was accompanied by people whom He had chosen especially to be helps ministers. Joanna and Susanna are mentioned here, along with many others, who served the Lord from out of their own means. In other words, there were people at that time—just as there are today—whose ministry was to supply the daily needs of Jesus and His disciples. They had real material needs; and so that they could do what they were meant to do, God made sure that these needs were met.

You must understand that Jesus had the same needs as any man, and that God satisfied His needs just as He does yours. Jesus needed sleep, rest, food and material goods to accomplish what He was called to do. These needs were met by the people around Him.

Jesus also had a treasurer. This, of course, implies that He had money, since He would hardly need a treasurer otherwise. In fact, He must have had so much money that He needed someone to manage it and keep financial matters properly in hand. Jesus did not appoint a treasurer because He did not want to defile or concern Himself with money, but because there was so much of it. This is a much more realistic view of Jesus.

Jesus also had the clothing that was practical and suitable for His needs. His robe, was a very expensive piece of clothing and not a bunch of old rags, and this was why the soldiers wanted it. They cast lots for it rather than divide it into four pieces, because it was a seamless garment.

If Jesus were alive on earth today, He would undoubtedly be wearing ordinary clothing just like everyone else. He was just like His fellow man at the time in which He lived. He had material needs, and by using other people, God was able to satisfy these needs.

Two Sides

You must understand the two sides of Jesus' life, otherwise you will be denying something that Jesus intended to bring blessing and freedom to your life.

Second Corinthians 8:2, describes the church in Macedonia, and says that, *Out of the most severe trial, their overflowing joy and their extreme poverty welled up in rich generosity* (NIV). Paul is saying here that they gave generously in spite of their circumstances and poverty which, in the natural, should have prevented them from doing so.

In this context, Paul uses two or three chapters of Second Corinthians to take up an offering for the saints in Jerusalem. He is exhorting the believers in Corinth to be a part of it. *I speak not by commandment,* he tells them, *but I am testing the sincerity of your love by the diligence of others* (2 Cor

8:8). To further emphasize the need to give, he uses Christ Jesus as an example.

For you know the grace of our Lord Jesus Christ, that though He was rich, yet for your sakes He became poor, that you through His poverty might become rich (2 Cor 8:9).

This poverty was expressed on the cross. As we have already mentioned, there are two distinct sides to the work of Jesus: His life on earth and His work on the cross. When the Bible talks about an act of substitution, it is referring to the cross. Our sin was exchanged for the righteousness of Jesus on the cross. It was there our death was exchanged for His life and our sickness was substituted for His healing.

Here we see that He became poor for our sakes so that through His poverty, that is, His work on the cross, we might become rich. This poverty is not referring to Jesus' walk on earth or suggesting that He had no food or clothing while He was here. That would have been of no benefit to us at all. Instead, it refers to the work of the cross, through which the resources of heaven, have now been made available to us.

Jesus hung on the cross naked, completely destitute and stripped of everything. He had surrendered everything there was to surrender. He gave all that He had in body, soul and spirit. What little clothing He had remaining was taken. He became truly poor on all levels; spiritually, mentally, physically and materially. As Paul says, "He became poor for our sakes that through His poverty we might become rich."

Notice that Paul did not hesitate to use the cross and the reconciliatory death of Jesus as an example of why the Corinthians should give money.

Jesus had all that He needed during His earthly walk. It was on the cross that He became poor. Your picture of Jesus needs to be correct, so that you can understand what He did for you and walk in it today.

7

The Rich Young Ruler—
What Did He Refuse?

We read about the story of the rich young ruler in Mark 10. We need to consider the entire context, since there are verses here that have often been used out of context. Jesus' words to the rich young ruler have been used by many, to claim that it is wrong for Christians to have many possessions. Some have made it a commandment for every Christian to follow: sell all that you own and then you can follow Jesus. But what is Jesus really saying here?

Let's start with verse 17, *Now as He was going out on the road, one came running, knelt before Him, and asked Him, "Good Teacher, what shall I do that I may inherit eternal life?"* This question came out of the man's feeling of unfulfillment, but he was not prepared to do what Jesus was about to tell him. Recognizing this, Jesus responded with a question to test his motives.

Why do you call Me good? No one is good but One, that is, God. You know the commandments: "Do not commit adultery," "Do not murder," "Do not steal," "Do not bear false witness," "Do not defraud," "Honor your father and your mother." And he answered and said to Him, "Teacher, all these I have kept from my youth." Then Jesus, looking at him loved him (vv. 18-21).

Jesus understood exactly where the man was. He saw that he was an honest man who wanted to do what was right. The dissatisfaction he felt inside caused him to approach Jesus, even though he was unprepared to really pay the price required. The scripture tells us here that Jesus loved him. For this reason He told him the truth, *"One thing you lack: Go your way, sell whatever you have and give to the poor, and you will have treasure in heaven."*

Don't Generalize!

A fundamental guideline in reading the Bible is to first understand the context of the scripture. Here Jesus is speaking to a rich young ruler. He is dealing with the specific problem of this young man. You do not necessarily have the same problem. Biblical situations are described primarily to illustrate or clarify a particular issue rather than a number of different issues. It can, however, be applied to various circumstances in your life.

What Jesus is telling this young man is not a general command. If it were, it would be included in the Sermon on the Mount or in the Great Commission, when Jesus was addressing a large number of people all at once.

Without this realization, it is easy to make a common mistake and draw the conclusion that you cannot follow Jesus unless you sell all you own and give it to the poor. This would imply that you are not following Jesus if you own material possessions!

The Bible tells us to let everything be confirmed by the mouth of two or three witnesses. Let scripture interpret itself. Let's look closely to see if Jesus really is saying that ownership in general is wrong. If so, Jesus is the first to fail the test, since we know that He had material possessions.

Sometimes problems can arise from personal testimonies in this area. People tend to make a law out of things they have heard from God personally, which have brought them freedom.

When God does speak to you, be sure to do *everything* He says. God wants to see the attitude of your heart. This was Jesus' intention with the rich young ruler. He was bound by his many possessions and Jesus told him:

"Sell whatever you have and give to the poor, and you will have treasure in heaven; and come, take up the cross, and follow Me." But he was sad at this word, and went away grieved, for he had great possessions (vv. 21-22). He was possessed by his possessions. He trusted in what he owned and, because he owned so much, he had difficulty leaving it all behind.

The True Meaning of Relinquishment

Relinquishment has its proper place in the life of the Christian, but it is primarily an attitude. It is not a question of getting rid of everything you own, it is simply a continual willingness to give. In this way you will remain free to do the will of God at all times. This is one aspect of relinquishment.

The other aspect is this; it always pays to relinquish. God does not expect you just to forsake something for no reason. Instead, He wants you to give up certain things so that He can give you something else in return! This is a side of the issue we have rarely considered.

We have previously described the meaning of a covenant. Two partners put themselves at one another's disposal and make their resources available to one another should such need arise.

This is the Biblical meaning of relinquishment: I place all my abilities and all that I have and am at God's disposal for Him to use whenever He wishes. He can do whatever He likes with me—with my mouth, my arms—with everything I have. In the same way, should I have need of His abilities or resources, these things have been put at my disposal. However, until I have placed myself at His disposal, I will be unable to make use of them.

This was the lesson Jesus wanted to teach the rich young ruler: If you sell your earthly possessions you will immediately receive a treasure in heaven. But just because your treasure is in heaven does not mean that you have to wait until you get to heaven to use it. It simply means that your treasure is kept in heaven for you. You have made a deposit into a heavenly rather than an earthly account.

The Bible says that you have been born into, *an inheritance incorruptible and undefiled and that does not fade away, reserved in heaven for you.* This heavenly treasure is undefiled by the moth and dust and inflation of this world—and it is available to you right now.

I can assure you that Jesus is speaking of nothing other than material goods to which you have access right here on earth. We need only read on in the same chapter to discover that these things are not just for when you get to heaven.

In the case of the rich young ruler, he first needed to get rid of the things that bound him so he could follow Jesus Christ. In doing so he would acquire a great treasure in heaven, a treasure that would be available to him on earth.

Then Jesus looked around and said to His disciples, "How hard it is for those who have riches to enter the kingdom of God!" (v. 23). Here, Jesus is showing how hard it is for those, who are owned by money, to enter God's Kingdom. The rich young ruler's problem was his bondage to money, although you can be bound by a career, by knowledge, by friends, etc. The more friends you have, the higher your status, the greater your income, the more bound you are—if you let yourself be bound.

The devil will use these things to tell you, "Just look at what you will lose if you get saved!" This is what makes it difficult for you to enter the Kingdom of God. However, Jesus never says that you will lose all these things by becoming a Christian. He offers a new set of priorities and a new way of life.

And the disciples were astonished at His words. But Jesus answered again and said to them "Children, how hard it is for those who trust in riches to enter the kingdom of God!" (Mark 10:23-24).

The disciples must have identified with the rich young ruler in some way. In other words, they did not consider themselves extremely poor, nor were they. Peter was by no means poor. He was a fisherman with others working for him. Neither was John's background one of poverty. He too was a fisherman who ran his father's company and he had important friends and relatives in the Jewish council.

But Jesus looked at them and said, "With men it is impossible, but not with God; for with God all things are possible" (v. 27). God is the one who saves people. If we are willing to let Him take this responsibility, anyone can be saved.

The Fruit of Relinquishment

A closer look at Mark chapter 10 will reveal that a large portion of the chapter is a single unit, in which the events take place in succession. We have often divided up the chapter and ended the story of the rich young ruler with verse 27 above. However, the account does not end there.

Let's look once again at what has happened. The rich young ruler approaches Jesus. Jesus speaks to him and he goes away saddened and grieved. The disciples wonder about the incident and Jesus begins to explain it. The disciples are astonished when Jesus tells them that it is difficult, or even impossible for a rich man to enter the Kingdom, but that for God, all things are possible.

Then Peter began to say to Him, "See, we have left all and followed You." Peter's implied meaning is, "What do we get out of it?" "Isn't that just like Peter," we think, "so fleshly and tactless!" But this reaction is a result of the fact that, unlike the disciples, we are unused to thinking in terms of a covenant.

The disciples, however, knew the meaning of a covenant; that it meant mutual obligation and responsibility. They could say with boldness, "We have done what you required, Jesus. We have given up everything and now we want to know what we get out of it."

It is possible that the disciples would have stayed with Jesus, even if He had told them that they had no reward. After all, they followed Him because they loved Him and believed He was the Messiah, not because they wanted a lot of things. At the same time, they understood the implications of a covenant and this was the motivation behind Peter's question.

I do not believe his question was carnal, nor that he was calculating the size of his reward.

So Jesus answered and said, "Assuredly, I say to you, there is no one who has left house or brothers or sisters or father or mother or wife or children or lands, for My sake and the gospel's, who shall not receive a hundredfold..." (vv. 29-30).

Perhaps you think this hundredfold is referring to the forgiveness of sins. After all, this is more important than anything else. No one would be foolish enough to trade their salvation for a car, or refuse to follow Jesus by saying, "I don't want to be saved, I'd rather hang onto my stuff."

This was exactly the rich young ruler's mistake. In his foolishness and ignorance he preferred corruptible riches which, would eventually break, rot or burn. The Bible tells us that everything we own will eventually disappear. Only three things are eternal: God, His Word and His people, and we should invest in these.

This man made a mistake by trying to invest in and preserve something he would eventually lose. Jesus told him that if he would do the opposite—by becoming less dependent on his worldly goods and willing to forsake them—then he would receive a hundredfold in return.

No bank in the world will give you such a good return on your investment. With a large sum of money and a high rate of interest, you might gain as much as 10-13%. However, Jesus says that when you give up something for Him, you will receive a hundred times as much in return!

Heaven—The Best Storehouse of All

Some people think we will receive this hundredfold in return, when we get to heaven. Certainly, it is worth forsaking everything in this present life to gain a treasure in heaven, but this is not what Jesus is saying. He says, *there is no one...who shall not receive a hundredfold now in this time* (see verses 29-30).

This reward does come from heaven, but we can begin to enjoy it in this present life! We do not need to go to heaven itself to receive what is there for us. The treasures of heaven have been made available to us right here and now. Heaven acts as our storehouse (see Deut 28:12).

> Blessed by the God and Father of our Lord Jesus Christ, who according to His abundant mercy has begotten us again to a living hope through the resurrection of Jesus Christ from the dead, to an inheritance incorruptible and undefiled and that does not fade away, reserved in heaven for you, who are kept by the power of God through faith for salvation ready to be revealed in the last time (1 Pet 1:3-5).

When we read this we may be inclined to think that although we have been born again and received a living hope, this hope is that when we get to heaven we will find an inheritance waiting for us there. However, this is not what the Bible says. These verses do not imply that you receive an inheritance only when you get to heaven.

The inheritance you have received is intended for both heaven and earth. It is referred to here as an incorruptible inheritance. It is an unending inheritance that remains pure and undefiled. You have not received it in an illegal manner. It is preserved for you in heaven, the best place you could possibly store something.

No thief is able to break in there and no one can steal what you have in heaven, that is, as long as you refuse to let the devil take what you have, by believing his lies. This is why Paul prays in Ephesians 1:17-23 that you will be given a spirit of revelation so that you might understand your inheritance in the saints.

We can better understand this by returning to Mark 10. *Assuredly, I say to you, there is no one who has left house or brothers or sisters or father or mother or wife or children or lands, for My sake and the gospel's, who shall not receive a hundredfold now in this time—houses* (He starts with material possessions) *and brothers and sisters and mothers and children and lands, with persecutions—and in the age to come, eternal life* (vv. 29-30).

Jesus says that you have an inheritance waiting for you in heaven. We have all heard that before, but we have not heard so much about the fact that this same inheritance is available to us right now. We can enjoy our inheritance in this life when we forsake what Jesus wants us to forsake.

A Hundredfold Return!

When we relinquish something in obedience to God—no matter what it may be—Jesus has promised that we will receive a hundredfold now, in this time. This is true whether it is brothers, sisters, mothers, children, lands or houses, including, of course, the contents of the house. This promise clearly applies to your worldly possessions. It also applies right in the middle of persecutions.

If you give up a house, then according to the Word of God—I am only reading what it says—you can expect a hundred in return. Perhaps you think I am being egotistical. The truth is, it is selfish not to want a hundred houses. There are people all over the world who could live in them. There are homeless children in India. Why not keep one for yourself and start children's homes in ninety-nine different countries with the others!

This is the point Jesus is trying to make: stop thinking only about yourself. Then you will see these principles come into operation on a continual basis.

Ecclesiastes 11:1 says, *Cast your bread upon the waters, for you will find it after many days.* You will always receive more than you have given and it will come to you in just about every possible means and from every possible direction. And it will be accompanied by persecutions.

The teaching of Jesus on relinquishment of material goods can, of course, be applied to other areas as well. For instance, if you are a preacher you might get your share of persecution and have a door shut in your face. But because you refuse to compromise your message, you will receive a hundredfold in this area. A hundred doors will be opened to you, all because you gave up one door to obey God.

Once I had to turn down an invitation to preach in a large European city. It was a painful decision, but I knew I had to stay at home and take care of administrative matters, something I am not particularly fond of. Just a few days later, an opportunity arose for me to preach on satellite television that would reach almost ten countries simultaneously.

When this happened, the Lord said to me, "I would not have been able to open this door for you if you had not turned down the other invitation." I was shocked to realize that it could be that sensitive.

Jesus shows us that for every situation in which you are willing to abandon and relinquish something, you will receive a hundredfold return. It is pure foolishness not to want to give up certain things. Only pride and prestige prevent believers from entering that supernatural flow in which they have access to God's resources and can fully enjoy their inheritance.

Jesus promises not only an abundant life when we get to heaven, He promises a hundredfold here, on earth. This applies not only to brothers, sisters, relatives, and those things we consider spiritual. Jesus actually starts His list with houses and finishes with lands, both of which are very tangible, material items.

What is really meant by calling something spiritual is that it comes from God. He *has blessed us with every spiritual blessing in the heavenly places in Christ* (Eph 1:3). The gnostic claims that all matter is evil, but the material things that God blesses, He calls good. If it comes from God you are to praise Him for it, without feeling guilty or ashamed.

After studying the story of the rich young ruler we understand that Jesus spoke directly into a particular situation. What He said, though, applies to those who are in the same situation even today. If this rich young ruler had given up all that he owned for the sake of Jesus and the Gospel, he would have become a hundred times richer.

This is, exactly what Jesus says afterwards. There is no one, not even the rich young ruler, with whom He has just finished speaking, who will not receive a hundredfold now, in this time.

Had the rich young ruler done what Jesus said, he would have received a hundredfold of all that he relinquished. He missed this opportunity because he did not understand the covenant. He failed to realize that Jesus was making him an offer that was far beyond any business proposal he had ever heard. There it was, right before his very eyes, but because of his greed he missed it completely. He held on to what he had, unaware of what he could have received.

Many people do precisely the same thing today. They say, "Don't count your chickens before they're hatched." However, this is a ridiculous attitude based purely on fear. The Bible says, *For whoever desires to save his life will lose it, but whoever loses his life for My sake and the gospel's will save it* (Mark 8:35).

This is the difference between fear and faith. Fear is stingy, afraid of the consequences and always trying to hold onto things. Fear must *see* before it can believe. On the other hand, faith is built on the knowledge of what God has promised. Therefore faith can easily release things. Abraham could easily give the most fertile part of the land to Lot because God had already pronounced, "The land is yours!" (see Gen 13:9).

Relinquishment is easy when you know what God has said. He has told you that whatever you give up will always return. You will receive exactly what He has promised to give. He will never forsake you, but will be with you to see that His promises are fulfilled in your life.

8

Allow God to Bless You!

We are all very different. When God wants to teach you how to walk in faith, He will begin in the area of your life where you are the most teachable. Your life is made up of several different "fields." God begins to work in those fields that are most fertile. However, His ultimate aim is to be able to work in every area of your life.

It is possible to walk in faith and be blessed in one field, while operating just like the world in another. For example, I may love Jesus and yet be extremely stingy. This is because I have not yet received teaching or revelation from the Word of God in this area. I have failed to realize that the same principle I use successfully in one area, can also be applied to the others.

*The just **shall live** by faith* (Rom 1:17). This is a principle that applies to every area of our lives, although it might take some time to see it in operation. This is because we have been brought up with the mentality of the world, poverty, greed and fear.

Of course, we should not be careless or wasteful. While we are to be wise stewards, we need also to be aware of the tendency to be governed by a spirit of poverty and bondage, which holds people captive. Many who want to save their finances for the Lord, do so out of unbelief and actually prevent the Lord from blessing them.

You need to make room for God in every area of your life. You glorify God by letting Him bless you. You may be a cheerful giver, but a poor receiver. God wants you to be able to receive, unashamedly. Give the glory to God, be thankful for what you receive and never feel guilty for what He gives you.

Who is it that receives the glory when you are blessed? God does, when you testify to everyone about what He has done. The devil, however, does not like this, so he keeps people captive in their poverty by saying that they should not be extravagant. However, it is worldly to think that you are being extravagant, because you are walking in the blessings of God.

Some people do not dare allow God to bless them for fear of what others might think. But when I receive something I thank God for it. I do not feel ashamed or embarrassed about it, but I do ask for the protection of the blood of Jesus from persecution.

Once, when the devil tried to attack me in this area, the Lord gave me a scripture that says, *The blessing of the Lord makes one rich, and He adds no sorrow with it* (Prov 10:22). I said to the Lord, "If this is indeed a blessing from you, then I refuse to accept a lot of worries, sorrows or attacks because of it. In the Name of Jesus, I ask for your protection!" As I prayed for divine protection the attack began to dissolve. God is good and He can ensure that what He gives us is preserved and protected.

God is not lacking to the extent that He is unable to meet your every need and desire. Your part is to receive it by faith and then to stand in faith for it. You need to work toward this and to be prepared for a few attacks as well. God wants you to be neither greedy nor to live in overindulgence. His only will is that you have what you need in abundance.

God Does Not Begrudge You Good Things

You must make up your mind to be willing to receive the blessings that God has for you, because along with the blessings will come persecutions. Following close behind the hundredfold blessings are the hundredfold envy and suspicion. But if you are secure in the fact that your attitude is right, you can praise God, regardless. There is nothing better than knowing that your conscience is clean.

When people begin to speculate and calculate how much money you earn and where it all comes from, it is important that your conscience is clean. It would be damaging to the Kingdom of God, not to mention embarrassing, if their accusations and suspicions turned out to be true after all.

God will bless you financially in the years to come. There is no limit to how much He will give you when you look after your affairs carefully and avoid being greedy or employing fleshly methods. The riches of this world belong to those with pure hands and the ability to manage these resources correctly.

God's desire is to entrust you with a great deal of money in the days ahead and to enable you to do what He has commanded. God blesses you for two primary reasons: partly because you are a steward and partly because you are His child. *If you then, being evil, know how to give good gifts to your children, **how much more** will your Father who is in heaven give good things to those who ask Him!* (Matt 7:11).

In any area of your life, the blessings of God are an expression of your Father's love and care for you as His child. Do not let lies cause you to begrudge yourself the good things God freely gives you. We are not talking about gloating over piles of money. This is not what it is all about. It is simply about receiving what God has for you. He allows you much more than even you allow yourself.

9

Paul's View of Money

In a previous chapter we dealt with what Jesus said about riches and ownership in the case of the rich young ruler. We understand that what He stated was to a particular person in a unique situation.

What Paul writes about money, however, is directed toward everyone. His writings are exhortations to the Church and are therefore intended for every believer. If the words of Jesus to the rich young ruler had been a general law or principle, Paul would have written the same thing in his letters, by revelation from God. But nowhere in his writings do we find a general command to all believers to give away all they own.

What does Paul say to those who are rich? His directions and exhortations are the Word of God, our yardstick and guide.

> Command those who are rich in this present age not to be haughty, nor to trust in uncertain riches but in the living God, who gives us richly all things to enjoy (1 Tim 6:17).

Never be so foolish as to put your trust in something as uncertain as riches. Do not put your trust in your checkbook. People have been known to commit suicide by jumping from windows in the midst of a financial catastrophe because they have placed their trust in money.

Just look at the resulting chaos if people's salaries do not come on time. This is true even of some

Christians, including those who supposedly preach faith. Down come their facades immediately and out goes their faith. As Paul says here, do not put your trust in uncertain riches, but in God, *who gives us richly all things to enjoy.*

Paul continues in verse 18 saying, *Command them to do good, to be rich in good deeds, and to be generous and willing to share* (NIV). This is to be the attitude of the rich. Notice that when Paul is exhorting the rich he does not tell them to sell all they own. Instead he says, "Just put your trust in the right thing, not in money, but in God who has given you what you have, for your enjoyment." Paul is not as religious as many of us seem to think!

There is nothing wrong with enjoying what you have. It is wrong only if this enjoyment becomes selfish and you begin to live for these things. There is a great difference between these two attitudes, and you must understand this, if you are to experience the life of victory and abundance God desires you to have.

It seems to be more difficult to explain these differences to journalists, to the world or to the religiously minded. You will understand the difference only if your life is led by the Holy Spirit. If you are led by your flesh, your understanding will be fleshly. But if you are led by the Spirit then you can be free to rejoice and enjoy what God has given you, using it both to give to others and to enjoy for yourself.

While you enjoy it, be sure to maintain a generous attitude and willingness to share with others. This is in accordance with the Word of God. Possessions are not wrong or dangerous. The wrong arises only when possessions have you! God gives you good gifts to bless you as His child and so that you in turn can bless others.

Money and Ministry

If you hold a position of ministry in the Kingdom of God you must do your utmost to walk before God with a clean conscience. Use a professional accountant to insure that financial matters are handled correctly.

As a servant of the Lord, you also need to be willing to go without a salary in certain situations and as the Lord directs. Paul often did so.

> Did I commit sin in humbling myself that you might be exalted, because I preached the gospel of God to you free of charge? I robbed other churches, taking wages from them to minister to you. And when I was present with you, and in need, I was a burden to no one, for what was lacking to me the brethren who came from Macedonia supplied. And in everything I kept myself from being burdensome to you, and so I will keep myself. As the truth of Christ is in me, no one shall stop me from this boasting in the regions of Achaia (2 Cor 11:7-10).

In other contexts Paul tells us that the worker is worthy of his hire and the ox should not be muzzled while treading out the grain. So what does he mean in the above passage? The Corinthians were very fleshly and Paul knew that they had money problems. Under the leading of the Holy Spirit he denied himself what was rightfully his.

The Bible tells us that a servant of the Gospel is to live from the Gospel; not from selling ads and insurance. It is the responsibility of the church to support him. In other words, a pastor or preacher has a full-time job and it is wrong to deprive the worker of his wages. However, situations may arise in which fleshly or unregenerate people cause us to act like Paul and go without payment.

This is what Paul is saying: "You are not my source, God is. My job is to preach the Gospel to you. But because you are so carnal that you fail to understand that you need to help me continue my travels, I refuse to take up an offering from you in case you say that I have plundered you and have taken your money. There are others who will support me."

When Paul planned to go to Rome he expected them to supply him for the rest of his journey. But such was not the case in Corinth. It was a church full of problems and he was forced to descend to their level.

The more you are used by the Lord, the wiser you need to be. Some people become wise by human standards and they compromise. We cannot allow ourselves to compromise in this area by showing regard for what others think. In delicate situations you must demonstrate wisdom and be led by the Holy Spirit.

If your conscience is clear it will not be easy for people to pin something on you. However, it will be quickly noticed if you are acting deceitfully with money. No one else may know about it, but it is noticeable in the spirit. You will experience diminished success and God will be dishonored.

Silencing Critics

As soon as we began the construction of our present facilities here at Word of Life, the real attacks started. Some journalists once asked me, "How much money do you make from your tapes?"

"Nothing," I answered.

Sudden silence followed. I have decided not to make any profit from the sale of cassette tapes. The money made from the many tapes we do sell is put toward the Gospel. We do not distribute tapes to make a profit, we do it to bless the people who are in need of our teaching. However, money is required to distribute cassette tapes. We have employees and equipment and increased expenses as a result of our new building.

"How much money have you made on this book?" one of them asked me, as he held up the book *Faith That Overcomes the World*.

"Nothing," I said. "It all goes to the building."

It became quiet again. They had asked the head of the publishing house the same question and received the same answer. Amazingly enough, this information actually made it into the newspaper, even though it contradicted previous reports.

It is wonderful to know that I have certain rights which, for the sake of the world and fleshly Christians, I have chosen to relinquish.

I receive a salary in my capacity as director, teacher and pastor of Word of Life. My goal is to decrease that income on a continual basis. The lower I keep my salary, the more I am forced to trust God. We are not to live by faith only until we get a fixed salary. You need to decide to live by faith the rest of your life.

Right now, I have to believe for more money than ever before. The previous sums I've had to believe for are nothing compared to these present ones. And the Lord continues to speak to us regarding new projects for which there is no financial covering in the natural.

Most recently, God spoke to us regarding a project to send 40 million Swedish kronor's worth of literature, videos and cassette tapes, as well as several full-time evangelists into the Soviet Union. We do not have that kind of money. Besides that, we have our own monthly expenses to cover. But we do not concentrate on meeting our own needs alone. We do what God has said by giving instead, knowing that He will supply our every need.

This is how we are to live. The Word of God tells us to be examples in word, in conduct, in love, in spirit, in faith and in purity (see 1 Tim 4:12). It must be apparent from our lives that we practice what we preach. People will be attracted when they see these things working for us. You need to keep yourself pure and continue to walk in faith in an area as sensitive as money. Sow out and just wait to see the resulting harvest. God will honor and bless you. He will protect, preserve and help you.

You Can Live by Faith

The first few seconds after an aircraft takes off are always the most dramatic. Once airborne, flying is easy. The same is true of your walk in the Spirit. You struggle feverishly to get off the ground, out of the natural realm and into the supernatural. Once there, you begin to feel at home. Your faith grows stronger and you see the devil defeated in one area after another. The promises of God are fulfilled in greater degree—you are flying.

Be of good cheer! God has performed financial miracles before. He loves to bring His people out of financial difficulties and set them free. The concrete, verifiable miracles of God are a tremendous testimony to others.

The revelation about financial prosperity cannot be stopped. When the people of God are finally free in this area, we will have what it takes to win the world.

God told Abraham that, through faith, the earth would be his inheritance (see Gen 12:1 and Heb 11:8). What we need today is deliverance from financial bondage. Poverty is a bondage, a kind of financial slavery from which Jesus has promised to deliver us. He came to set the captives free, including those bound financially.

Jesus brought the Good News to the poor. What is good news for the poor? Riches and prosperity, of course. And, praise the Lord, this same Good News is for us! We have no right to waste these resources or spend them on our fleshly passions, but we will do with them exactly what God desires—take the world for the Gospel.

Contentment Is the Key

Our attitude should be like Paul's: "I am willing to give things up. I do not always have to receive." It is pathetic to see people who should be serving God, clutching for money. This kind of begging happens all over the world.

Paul warns against this sort of attitude: *useless wranglings of men of corrupt minds and destitute of the truth, who suppose that godliness is a means of gain* (1 Tim 6:5). Such people think it possible to make money from godliness. Unfortunately, there are such people today. They have discovered a way

to make money from God and they deceive
themselves with their cunning sales tactics. It is
sickening to meet such individuals whose impurity
is easily conspicuous.

Ephesians 5:3 says that fornication, uncleanness
or covetousness are not even to be mentioned among
us. God hates covetousness. It prevents people from
walking in His blessings. In First Timothy 6:6 Paul
says, *But godliness with contentment is great gain.*
Contentment is an attitude that, is independent of
how much you have. The key to receiving more is
being content with what you already have.

Godliness with contentment is a position in which
I want nothing more than to fear and serve God. I
am not out to get something. I want only to please
God. Along this line, Psalm 75 tells us that exaltation
comes from the Lord. God uses those who are content
rather than those who are idly waiting for their big
"chance" or "breakthrough."

In First Timothy 6:7-8 Paul goes on to say, *For
we brought nothing into this world, and it is certain
that we can carry nothing out. And having food and
clothing, with these we shall be content.*

**The key to success is fellowshipping with
God and being content.**

This was Paul's attitude and it is the prerequisite
for the Christian life. "And having food and clothing,
with these we shall be content." Some people have
tried to twist this verse to mean that we are allowed
nothing more than the absolute essentials in life.
However, this is not what Paul is saying. He is
referring to an attitude of contentment.

Later in the same chapter Paul says that God
has blessed the rich with all things for their
enjoyment. He is not being inconsistent. He is

demonstrating the importance of the right outlook on riches. Do not start "standing in faith" to get other people's things. This is nothing more than coveting your neighbor's goods.

But those who desire to be rich fall into temptation and a snare, and into many foolish and harmful lusts which drown men in destruction and perdition. For the love of money is a root of all kinds of evil, for which some have strayed from the faith in their greediness, and pierced themselves through with many sorrows (1 Tim 6:9-10).

Paul does not say that money itself is the root of all evil. There are certain ideologies that make this claim but the Bible is diametrically opposed to such a view. The Word of God is clear on this: there is nothing wrong with money or possessions. It is the *love* of money that is a root of all kinds of evil. Those who are driven by the desire and lust for money and possessions will be led astray from the faith and will pierce themselves with many sorrows.

If people grasp the message of financial prosperity for the sake of selfish gain, according to the Bible, they will pierce themselves through with many sorrows. It is impossible to get this teaching to work by living in the flesh. Your attitude must first be right.

Money and the Government

Let's read now in Ephesians 4:28: *Let him who stole steal no longer....* Stealing is an external manifestation of greed. There are many different ways in which to steal. You can break a shop window and take the goods inside, or you can do it in a more sophisticated manner. You can cheat with income taxes, make false deductions or call things by another name when submitting a declaration.

I have no right to say, "The state has stolen so much from me that I have a right to take some of it back." The Bible tells us to pay taxes. When you pay your taxes, praise God and say:

"This is the money the state says I owe. I give it to them willingly. No one is taking it from me. God, I ask that this money be used for sensible purposes and not to finance the work of the devil. My money will be used to further the work of God. It will be used for the good of the people; for hospitals, help for the handicapped and so one. In the Name of Jesus I bless my tax contribution. I set it apart for the expansion of the Kingdom of God through the system of taxation."

Doing this will make you stop complaining about your taxes. Of course, you can continue to pray for more justice in the system, but until that day comes, you still have to pay your taxes.

Let him who stole steal no longer, but rather let him labor, working with his hands what is good, that he may have something to give him who has need (Eph 4:28).

According to the Bible, working should give you enough money to meet both your needs and the needs of others.

If you are living in a society with a tax system which makes it impossible for you to have enough left over to give to others, you need to pray for the Lord to change that system. It is God's will that you have enough to give to others.

10

God Is Your Provider

God is the God of abundance. He is a rich God and He meets your needs according to His riches in glory, in Christ Jesus. All that God gives, comes to us in and through Jesus Christ. The blessings mentioned in this book are yours dependent on the fact that you are under the New Covenant and because of what Jesus has done for you.

Let's continue now to study what Paul had to say about God's provision for His children and the attitude He desires us to have in the financial area. In Philippians 4:10-19 Paul says:

> But I rejoiced in the Lord greatly that now at last your care for me has flourished again; though you surely did care, but you lacked opportunity. Not that I speak in regard to need, for I have leaned in whatever state I am, to be content: I know how to be abased, and I know how to abound. Everywhere and in all things I have learned both to be full and to be hungry, both to abound and to suffer need. I can do all things through Christ who strengthens me. Nevertheless you have done well that you shared in my distress. Now you Philippians know also that in the beginning of the gospel, when I departed from Macedonia, no church shared with me concerning giving and receiving but you only. For even in Thessalonica you sent aid once and again for my necessities. Not that I seek the gift, but I seek the fruit that abounds to your account. Indeed I have all and abound. I am full, having received from Epaphroditus the things which were sent from you, a sweet-smelling aroma, an acceptable sacrifice,

well pleasing to God. And my God shall supply all your need according to his riches in glory by Christ Jesus.

Be Content—But Not Passive!

We often hear people saying, "We shouldn't talk so much about money. We should be content with what we have. After all, didn't the apostle Paul say that he was content in every circumstance?" Those who say this are taking this scripture directly out of context.

For many of us, the word "content" carries with it the implication of passivity. However, this is not what it means in the Bible. In Greek, the word "content" means "self-sufficient" or "self-producing." When Paul was content in every situation, it meant that he was self-sufficient; that regardless of his circumstances, he knew God was more than enough to produce what he needed.

Paul points out two different pitfalls, which we should avoid. On the one hand is greed, coveting your neighbor's goods and never being content with what you have.

The other pitfall is believing that contentment means being happy with what you have to the extent that you never try to get anything more. But can you imagine telling a newborn infant to be content with what he has? He has nothing. We enter this world with nothing and we leave with nothing. It is while we are *in* this world that we need things. Material blessings are designed to help you live in this world.

Paul is talking about this *attitude* when he says that he has no lack. He had learned to be content in every circumstance. Occasionally, he found himself in situations where he was in lack and suffered need. He said, *I have learned both to be full and to be hungry, both to abound and to suffer need* (v 12).

Paul encourages the Philippians, however, telling them, *Nevertheless you have done well that you shared in my distress* (v 14). He refers to need and hunger as distress. He does not call these things blessings. He does not tell us that going without food and clothing and shelter for a couple of days is wonderful or enjoyable. He calls it distress, though he knew how to respond to it when it came.

In other words, Paul was saying, "It was good of you to send me some money. I know what it is like to be poor as well as rich (and being rich is better!)." This is exactly what he is explaining: I have suffered need and I have abounded, and abounding is clearly better.

If you read in Second Corinthians 11:22-23 along with several portions of the book of Acts, you will quickly discover that there were periods in Paul's life when he suffered need. He was attacked, shipwrecked and subjected to many forms of misery. Paul had learned to be content in every situation because he knew that God was his provider. His expectation was not in people or circumstances, His expectation was in God.

The primary key to walking in financial prosperity is never to look at people as your source of provision. Christian ministries and religious organizations often expect people to take on this responsibility. Then, when the money fails to come in they pressurize these people to provide.

God Uses People

If God is truly your provider rather than people, you can be unmoved and content in any circumstance. Your trust is where it should be—in the Lord.

Philippians 4:10-19 is actually a revelation of the nature of God. Paul assures the church in Philippi, *And my God shall supply all your need according to His riches in glory by Christ Jesus.* In other words, Paul is saying, "God has always met my needs. I know Him personally. *He* is my provider, not people." We see from these scriptures that one important aspect of walking in financial prosperity is being free from dependency on other people.

On the other hand, God has made other people to be channels through which He provides money. Material blessings always come to us via others.

There is a difference between finances and healing, for instance. Sometimes, God uses other people as channels to bring healing, but not always. Healing can occur through the laying on of hands or it can come directly from God.

However, when it comes to finances, God always uses other people as His channels. He does not have a mint in heaven. Through the Holy Spirit, He is able to direct money by way of other people to reach selected targets here on earth.

Luke 6:38 says, *Give, and it shall be given unto you.* You will always receive back when you give. It is a spiritual law. What you give will be given back to you, and you will always get back more than you have given.

How do we receive? *Good measure, pressed down, and shaken together, and running over, shall men give into your bosom* (KJV). The word "men" here means people. Jesus says that when you give to God, people are the channels through which you will receive your reward. See yourself as a channel and keep that channel open so God can flow through you in the way He desires.

Trust God to meet your needs. He is your ultimate source. You never need to beg others for money. Simply trust God that the Holy Spirit will prompt those people whom He has called to give.

Paul was like this. I am convinced that he went first to God with His needs and asked Him to send someone to help him, allowing God to decide how and by whom it would be done.

Free From Worry

God has called you to walk in faith. However, this does not mean that you are to quit your job. That would be foolishness rather than faith. You should not begin to think about taking such a step until you have so much to do in ministry that your job becomes a hindrance.

When you leave a fixed salary behind you will soon discover that God will give you more through other means than you ever received from the more traditional sources of salary and employment. Work is just a *means* by which the Lord can provide you with money. There are countless other sources through which the Lord can meet your needs. It is not up to you to decide the source of the money, leave that up to God.

When you lack money, when your expenses exceed your income, you are in need of a financial miracle. Do not, at this point, pray, "Father, I praise you that my mother will notice my worn out clothes and give me two hundred dollars." Some people try to figure out different ways to demonstrate their needs so that people will give. This is called worry and anxiety and it is a sin.

In the Sermon on the Mount, Jesus reveals that serving mammon is synonymous with worrying about material things.

> No one can serve two masters; for either he will hate the one and love the other, or else he will be loyal to the one and despise the other. You cannot serve God and mammon. *Therefore* I say to you, do not worry about your life, what you will eat or what you will drink; nor about your body, what you will put on (Matt 6:24-25).

It is extremely interesting to notice the connection Jesus is making here. It is not those who are rich who serve mammon, He says, it is those who *worry* about how to get material things. Why? Jesus goes on to describe how carefully the Father feeds the birds of the air and clothes the lilies of the field, although these things are not eternal. If God takes such care of His "lower" creatures, Jesus continues, how much more will He not meet the needs of man, the crown of His creation?

We, are experts at worrying. We are used to living in a world in which things can be seen, experienced and felt. When you see that your bank balance includes a certain number of zeros, you feel happy and secure. However, when you receive a bill that exceeds the number of zeros on your statement, suddenly your money is gone and your joy along with it. This is called walking according to sight and circumstances and it is something you cannot afford to do.

God is not against you feeling happy about your bank account, but you must release yourself from dependency on your visible resources. This can take time. You need to begin by meditating on what the Word of God has to say about this area until it becomes a personal conviction in your heart. As a result, God will set you free from the financial bondage and fear in which most people are still caught.

People lie awake at night. They count and calculate, and some even go as far as to commit suicide because they cannot pay their bills. It is a terrifying bondage—but just as God has a solution for all of our problems, He has a solution for this one too.

God's answer to the problem of financial bondage is financial prosperity through Jesus Christ. But before it can become a reality in your life, you must get to the point where you personally learn to walk by faith in this area. Turn your attention away from what you see in front of you and stop worrying.

Be anxious for nothing, but in everything by prayer and supplication, with thanksgiving, let your requests be made known to God; and the peace of God, which surpasses all understanding, will guard your hearts and minds through Christ Jesus. Finally, brethren, whatever things are true, whatever things are noble, whatever things are just, whatever things are pure, whatever things are lovely, whatever things are of good report, if there is any virtue and if there is anything praiseworthy—meditate on these things (Phil 4:6-8).

Never Let Money Decide!

Those who are pastors need to be on their guard against allowing people with financial resources to control them. The book of James warns against showing favoritism toward the rich over the poor (see Jas 2:1-4). Just because someone is a rich businessman does not automatically make him spiritually in tune. Similarly, a pastor is not necessarily good at business. He can receive powerful revelation without knowing anything about money.

A giver should never be allowed to lead a minister or a church. The amount of money a person has says nothing about their influence in the spirit realm. Something has gone terribly wrong when money begins to direct a church. God never intended money to lead His Church, He intended the Holy Spirit to lead it.

Many people are motivated by a desire for personal influence or power. You cannot ever afford to be influenced by such people. If you are, you will be prevented from doing the will of God.

You must stay free by spending time in your prayer closet and by walking in faith in the area of personal finances. Your personal victory will be transferred to your public ministry, where you may later be dealing with large sums of money. The principles of prosperity stay the same, regardless of the amount you are dealing with.

It is important to stay pure and free in the area of money. You may end up dealing with a lot of it. We are living at a time when God will supernaturally release resources across the earth to finance the mighty work that needs to be accomplished. You must be a ready and clean channel, if what He desires to do through you is to be fulfilled.

Keep the Vision Clear

Just as all of us can be attacked with physical sickness, it is possible to be attacked financially. This does not mean that we are sinners or that God has forsaken us. We are merely under attack. During these times, it is vital to remember that this is not a permanent condition.

If you find yourself in a time of famine, but continue to "sow" and apply the Biblical principles, you will emerge on the other side victoriously. Do not become afraid when you are attacked. Rather than worry, present your requests before God with prayer, petitions and thanksgiving.

Praise God in such situations for complete and total victory and for a way of escape from temptation. Like Paul, you will be able to say, "I know what it is to abased and I know what it is like to abound. I can be content and confident in any position or circumstance. I can be hungry. I can be fed. I can have abundance and I can suffer lack. In other words, I can handle any situation because I can do all things through Him who strengthens me."

Paul was saying that he was not dependent on anyone to do what God had called him to do. He was not dependent on his circumstances. He could handle anything. Though he had only a wooden plank on the open sea, he was determined to reach the emperor in Rome—and because this was his attitude, he made it.

Just imagine what would have happened if Paul had said, "Unless I cross the Mediterranean in a luxury liner and stop off at Crete, the trip is off." Instead, in spite of how he got there, he had made up his mind to see the Roman emperor.

Remarkably enough, it was the state that paid his way. As a prisoner, Paul was provided with food, clothing, transportation and protection throughout his journey. He had everything he needed, including protection from those who wanted to take his life. His provision was ideal for the situation. However, the devil still tried to use a shipwreck to stop him. But Paul walked in his royal authority as a king and priest before God, even as a prisoner, and so the entire ship was saved, and he reached Rome.

We are also on a journey, and possessions cannot be allowed to prevent us from reaching our destination. We do not live only for ourselves. With this attitude, it is easy to make an offering. The vision God has given us ought to be so central to our lives that we refuse to retreat, even when our flesh reacts.

God is the God of abundance. His plans and intentions are already blessed. Of course, you must pray, stand in faith and drive back the powers of darkness.

The channels need to be open and able to carry the means to finance what God has instructed you to do. The devil may try to block these channels so you need to fight in the spirit and keep the victory. However, do not go crawling to others begging for money or trying to use flattery to talk them into giving. If God has decided to do something, it has been blessed and He will assure that it happens.

11

Sowing and Reaping

But this I say: He who sows sparingly will also reap sparingly, and he who sows bountifully will also reap bountifully. So let each one give as he purposes in his heart, not grudgingly or of necessity; for God loves a cheerful giver. And God is able to make all grace abound toward you, that you, always having all sufficiency in all things, have an abundance for every good work. As it is written, "He has dispersed abroad, He has given to the poor; His righteousness remains forever." Now may He who supplies seed to the sower, and bread for food, supply and multiply the seed you have sown and increase the fruits of your righteousness, while you are enriched in everything for all liberality, which causes thanksgiving through us to God (2 Cor 9:6-11).

Here Paul reminds us of the law of sowing and reaping. This law always operates in proportion and according to how much you give. The more you sow, the greater your harvest. You will personally reap what you have sown. The crop will be the same, but the amount will be greater. Galatians 6:8 tells us that we will reap corruption if we sow to the flesh, but eternal life if we sow to the Spirit.

You Reap What You Sow

Whether you sow your time, your money or something else, you will always reap the same thing that you sow. This is how it works in the natural: parsley seed does not produce carrots. It is impossible. What you put in the ground is exactly what comes up.

Another facet of this law is that some crops grow quickly, while others take more time. This can be both good and bad. The person who plants an olive tree seldom lives long enough to pick an olive from that same tree. In this case it is the next generation that will reap what the previous one has planted. Certain things bring long-term results, while other things produce a quick, but unenduring return.

When you plant or sow something, it is better to find a seed that continues to produce fruit for a long period of time. For example, you will benefit more from the seed of an apple tree than from the seed of a radish. God has provided you with long-term areas in which to sow and He will show you exactly what they are.

Paul tells us that he who sows sparingly will also reap sparingly. But to encourage you, he promises: *And God is able to make all grace abound toward you, that you, always having all sufficiency in all things, have an abundance for every good work.* Here, God is saying that He is the giver and you are the sower. He supplies seed to the sower and bread for food. If you dare to place yourself at His disposal and begin to give, this law will come into operation.

We need to remember two important laws: the law of sowing and reaping and the law of faith, or walking by what is not seen. You must always walk in faith. You need to exercise this faith by beginning to sow what little seed you have.

Take a step of faith at a time when you personally have very little to give, and sow. You must begin somewhere if this law is to function for you. At a time of need it is easy to think that you ought to hold on to what you have. The mentality of the world says, "Keep what you have. Don't let anyone else have it." However, the Kingdom of God is the opposite of this.

Dare to Give

There is one who scatters, yet increases more; And there is one who withholds more than is right, But it leads to poverty. The generous soul will be made rich, And he who waters will also be watered himself. The people will curse him who withholds grain, But blessing will be on the head of him who sells it (Prov 11:24-26).

This law works. If you dare to test it, God will give you more blessings than you have room to contain.

Make a quality decision to always do what God tells you to do. Every time you wonder if you can afford it, you are asking your checkbook for permission. If God says yes and your checkbook says no, do it anyway. On the other hand, you should not do something if God says no, even if your checkbook says yes. Be led by the Holy Spirit and not your bank balance!

You may find yourself in a situation where you have nothing. God does not condemn you or complain about you. He looks at your will. If your will is engaged and you give according to your present ability, you will end up "giving" yourself out of famine and into prosperity.

Some people, however, stop giving as soon as they receive some money. Their resources dry up and suddenly, that money has disappeared—all because they tried to retain it. What you attempt to hold on to will always disappear.

Do not delay if God exhorts you to sow into a particular project. When the Holy Spirit speaks, you should be prepared to sow within a second's notice. This will bring you out of financial bondage and into freedom, where God wants every one of us. If you lack money at the moment, God will provide it for you. There is no greater satisfaction than to give to the work of God. It involves being independent of the world and having the freedom to act and do what God has told us to do.

Sow into Good Soil

When Paul exhorts the Corinthians to contribute to the collection for the poor in Jerusalem, he uses the substitutionary death of Jesus as a motivation for them to give. According to Paul, the reason they should give is because Christ Jesus Himself became poor so that, through His poverty, they might become rich and therefore able to give:

> For you know the grace of our Lord Jesus Christ, that though he was rich, yet for your sakes He became poor, that you through His poverty might become rich. And in this I give advice: It is to your advantage not only to be doing what you began and were desiring to do a year ago; but now you also must complete the doing of it; that as there was a readiness to desire it, so there also may be a completion out of what you have. For if there is first a willing mind, it is accepted according to what one has, and not according to what he does not have. For I do not mean that others should be eased and you burdened; but by an equality, that now at this time your abundance may supply their

lack, that their abundance also may supply your lack—that there may be equality (2 Cor 8:9-14).

Always sow your seed into good soil and never sow under pressure. God will speak to you, thus enabling you to give with joy. However, do not give an arbitrary sum. Ask God how much you are to give.

The devil does not want believers to give. If they do, he wants them to contribute to the wrong things. If you sow into something that is not approved by God, the devil has channeled your money down a blind alley and prevented it from bearing fruit. You should do nothing out of routine or religious duty, but let it flow as a result of your fellowship with the Lord. In this way, you will be actively involved in what God is doing.

Similarly, you should not allow threats or flattery to motivate your giving as this is not the leading of the Holy Spirit either. As soon as you feel under pressure to give, stop immediately. This is not the correct motivation for giving—and the motivation for giving is the most critical issue.

The sum of money is not what matters. This is what Paul is saying: *For if the willingness is there, the gift is acceptable according to what one has, not according to what he does not have* (NIV). God does not consider the amount of money given, He looks at the motive behind the giving.

Stick to Your Decision!

Paul wanted to remind the believers in Corinth of their previous decision. Like the rest of us, they had a tendency to act on impulse and then go home and forget all about it. Now, a year later, Paul was writing to remind them of their decision. He says,

Now finish the work, so that your eager willingness to do it may be matched by your completion of it, according to your means (NIV).

If you have made a decision before God to contribute to a particular cause, that is, if you have made a financial promise, it is too late to try and excuse yourself by saying that you have nothing to give. It is not a question of what you have, it is a question of what you promised. If you do have nothing, then give according to what you do have!

Prove that you are willing to carry out your decision. God considers the promise you made to be sacred and precious. Just as His promises to us are precious, He wants the promises we make to be equally precious, holy and reliable.

God is merciful. He fully understands your situation and will never condemn you. He sees your good will and intentions. But you should make sure you do not forget to do what you have promised. There are two important sides to this issue: On the one hand, we must be sure to keep our promises and, on the other hand, we must avoid getting into legalistic bondage by letting others force us into making wrong decisions and doing things we would otherwise never do.

God has established a financial plan for His Kingdom and it involves us giving voluntarily to His work. This is a ministry to the Lord, which is no less holy than praise and worship in the Spirit.

12

Prosperity in Every Area of Life

Beloved, I pray that you may prosper in all things and be in health, just as your soul prospers (3 John 2).

John was inspired by the Holy Spirit when he wrote this. God's will is communicated here, not just a general greeting from John himself.

To prosper "in all things" refers to prosperity in every area of your life. Money is just one of these areas. The message of financial prosperity is only one aspect of the complete prosperity God desires to give you. God is a God of prosperity. He is a covenant God. Because of the covenant He has made with you, He wants to meet your every need. And He meets your needs with His abundance and prosperity.

A life of prosperity means having so much, that not only are your own needs met, but you can also meet the needs of others.

Adam had no lack in the Garden of Eden. He never experienced any need because God was his constant source of provision.

Jesus Christ said that He had come to give abundant life: *The thief does not come except to steal, and to kill, and to destroy. I have come that they may have life, and that they may have it more abundantly* (John 10:10). The thief comes to steal many things—and among them is your money. Jesus, however, came to give us abundant life, and this means having an unlimited supply.

Financial prosperity is the lowest level of this abundant life. While it is not to be despised, you need to recognize that life with God is much more than a couple of dollar bills in your pocket. Money is the world's ultimate guarantee of a secure life. For us, that guarantee is God.

Think Right!

Prosperity involves every aspect of your life. God wants you to have an abundance of peace, joy, power and love. He has deposited these within you. However, the spirit and the flesh are continually at war within you, and there is a struggle against the devil, who is out to steal your strength, your peace, your health and even your possessions.

Just as God wants you to prosper, the devil wants you to fail. He often uses fear, coupled with the power of association, to achieve this. You see the unrighteous and their riches and conclude that having what they have, would automatically make you unrighteous.

God is your defense. When you are blessed materially, those who are spiritual will listen to what the Holy Spirit has to say about it. Such people will never cause you problems. On the other hand, fleshly people, who respond to what the carnal mind says, will always cause you trouble.

You need to maintain an attitude of humility and a willingness to adjust to every situation. But be sure to let God be the one who adjusts you, not the devil. Satan would like to make you look truly "spiritual" by getting you to "forsake" everything.

In certain situations Jesus tells us to be prepared to forsake everything. He once said to His disciples, "Whoever desires to come after me, let him deny himself." He is referring to an attitude of heart. We cannot follow Jesus if our lives are directed and bound by something such as houses or other earthly possessions. If you have so much as a thought that says, "I can't follow the Lord because I don't want to lose my car or my house and so on," then Jesus is speaking to you. You cannot follow Him. You are not worthy of Him.

Although you must always be prepared to give things up, the devil has often used this scripture to point the finger at you and say, "You have to get rid of everything before you can serve Jesus!" However, what Jesus is talking about has nothing to do with immediately giving up everything you own, but simply with your willingness to do so if He requires it. Nothing should be allowed to stop you from following God.

You must make up your mind once and for all that all your money, your possessions and your time belongs to Jesus. The Holy Spirit will then lead you as to how and when you are to give.

As we mentioned earlier, there are times when God directs us to go without certain things. However, there is no arbitrary rule governing this. It is crucial to be led by the Holy Spirit. He will tell you what you are to relinquish and your decision will be accompanied by peace and joy. Remember that you do not live only for yourself!

Think Further!

You must choose to follow the Word of God. If you have received revelation from God's Word regarding financial prosperity, He wants you to obey His Word, by walking in that revelation.

If God has said, "I have determined to bless you," and you respond by saying that you do not want to be blessed, you are in disobedience.

If you think that prosperity is unimportant and that it is up to you to decide how much money you should have and what you will do with it, you are thinking selfishly. You are afraid of persecution and afraid that people will speak evil of you. In fact, you are being egotistical, and have failed to realize that prosperity involves more than your personal needs. Although it may begin there, prosperity is God revealing to you the way in which His resources should be distributed throughout the earth.

It is your responsibility to make sure that you secure the good things God has promised you and that you use them according to the leading of the Holy Spirit. Sometimes, you need to make a difficult decision—allow yourself to be blessed!

When Jesus came to live and dwell in you, He brought with Him all the resources of heaven. You have access to these things. Is that anything to be ashamed of? No, God would rather that you brag about His blessings. The Bible says, *Let him who boasts boast in the Lord* (2 Cor 10:17 NIV). You should boast about the blessings of God.

God wants you to testify to His blessings in every area of your life. There is a spiritual force that would like to tell us that ownership is evil. It is the spirit of Antichrist because it is in opposition to the Word of God. The Bible guards and protects the right to private ownership and this is an area in which God wants you to be blessed.

Abraham was a rich man who walked continually in the blessings of God. However, when he was presented with an opportunity to gain possessions unjustly, he refused to receive them, and thus avoided being brought into bondage (see Gen 14:23).

God will bless you if you have the right motives. It all starts with you receiving this teaching and understanding that it is not just about your personal gain. Prosperity exists for the expansion of God's Kingdom. The Gospel can be spread to the ends of the earth—through financial freedom.

Other Books by Ulf Ekman

A Life of Victory
The guidance, help and inspiration you need to put God's
Word first. Fifty-four chapters, each dealing with a
particular area of the believer's life. 288 pages

The Authority in the Name of Jesus
When you receive a revelation of what the name of Jesus
really means, you will have boldness like never before.
Booklet, 32 pages

Destroy the Works of the Devil
Jesus came to earth to destroy the works of the devil.
His death on the cross struck Satan a death blow. Jesus
triumphed over him and won the victory for YOU.
Booklet, 32 pages

Faith that Overcomes the World
Explains how faith arises, how it becomes operational,
and what makes it grow. 144 pages

God, the State and the Individual
God not only deals with individuals, but with nations
and governments. You can change the destiny of your
nation! 112 pages

God Wants to Heal Everyone
Discover the wonderful fact that God's will is to heal
everyone—including you. Booklet, 32 pages

Power in the New Creation
A new dimension of victorious living awaits you. The
Lord is with you, Mighty Warrior! Booklet, 32 pages

The Jews—People of the Future
Clarifies basic truths about the people and the land.
Historical facts and Biblical prophecies combine to reveal
the fulfillment of God's End-time Plan. 160 pages

The Prophetic Ministry
*"Provides essential guideposts for the operation of the
prophetic ministry today."* From the Foreword by Demos
Shakarian. 224 pages

Available from your local Christian bookstore, or order
direct from the publisher:

Word of Life Publications
Box 17, S-751 03 Uppsala, Sweden
Box 46108, Minneapolis, MN 55446, USA
Box 641, Marine Parade, Singapore 9144